THE

UFO

FILES

Palmiro Campagna

The UFO Files
The Canadian Connection Exposed

DUNDURN PRESS
TORONTO

Library and Archives Canada Cataloguing in Publication

Campagna, Palmiro
   The UFO files : the Canadian connection exposed / Palmiro Campagna.

Includes bibliographical references and index.
ISBN 978-1-55488-699-9

   1. Unidentified flying objects--Sightings and encounters--Canada. 2. Unidentified flying objects.
I. Title.

TL789.6.C3C36 2010   001.9420971   C2009-906741-2

1 2 3 4 5   14 13 12 11 10

 Conseil des Arts du Canada   Canada Council for the Arts   Canadä    ONTARIO ARTS COUNCIL CONSEIL DES ARTS DE L'ONTARIO

We acknowledge the support of the Canada Council for the Arts and the Ontario Arts Council for our publishing program. We also acknowledge the financial support of the Government of Canada through the Book Publishing Industry Development Program and The Association for the Export of Canadian Books, and the Government of Ontario through the Ontario Book Publishers Tax Credit program, and the Ontario Media Development Corporation.

Care has been taken to trace the ownership of copyright material used in this book. The author and the publisher welcome any information enabling them to rectify any references or credits in subsequent editions.

J. Kirk Howard, President

Printed and bound in Canada.
www.dundurn.com

Dundurn Press
3 Church Street, Suite 500
Toronto, Ontario, Canada
M5E 1M2

Gazelle Book Services Limited
White Cross Mills
High Town, Lancaster, England
LA1 4XS

Dundurn Press
2250 Military Road
Tonawanda, NY
U.S.A. 14150

For Adrian Philip

and all those who seek truth;
may you keep an open yet objective mind
lest you follow in the path of naivete

Contents

Preface to the Paperback Edition

The publication of this new edition has given me the opportunity to update some long-standing UFO controversies. In this Preface and in the Postscript, I give new information based on interviews I have conducted recently with people directly involved in alleged UFO activities. In the Appendix, I provide additional documents and new illustrations that authenticate Canadian involvement in UFO research.

June 1997 marked the fifty-year anniversary of the now infamous Roswell incident (when a UFO allegedly crashed near the town of Roswell, New Mexico, and was subsequently recovered by the U.S. military). The town of Roswell put on quite the celebration, reported in all the papers, and on television and radio. Unfortunately, though, the much-anticipated release of new information proving the extraterrestrial nature of the incident never came. Instead, the U.S. government tried to ruin the party by releasing new denials and explanations for what happened there. Details are included in the Postscript.

However, it is worth mentioning here that the black-and-white alien autopsy footage received greater attention at the 1997 Roswell party. One idea being advanced is that this autopsy film is not the original, but is actually a copy. This fact would make it even more difficult to determine the film's authenticity, a debate that continues to this day. The cameraman has since provided some covert interviews to a Japanese television crew, but his identity remains a closely guarded secret by Ray Santilli, the man who made the autopsy film public. Is the cameraman telling the truth? Will he ever step out of the shadows? And what is to be made of the existence of a short film-clip that shows the alleged interrogation of an alien? Is the clip real or staged?

Perhaps the most interesting piece of information has come in the form of a new book, *The Day after Roswell*, by Col. Phillip J. Corso. In the book, published in 1997, Corso claims to have had access to some of the Roswell wreckage and to have provided it to industry over the course of several years in order to help give the technological edge to the United States. For example, Corso claims credit for advancing the development of the microchip (by reverse engineering alien technology), the laser, and a host of other developments. It is a most interesting account and, if true, a startling one. Unfortunately, Corso does not provide any hard evidence — no documents to speak of or other materials. Corso has only his word and stature to offer. Still, his matter-of-fact style of explaining what happened is compelling.

In my own ongoing research, which I present in the Postscript, I have uncovered material concerning Wilbert Smith, the Department of Transport employee who was told by an American scientist back in 1950 that the UFOs were real. In addition, I have discovered a previously unreported North American Air Defence Agreement (NORAD) case. I provide some additional insight into the Michalak case, in which a witness approached and was subsequently burned by a UFO when it took off. And I have added to the illustration section more strange experimental craft from the USAF and some additional documents outlining the Canadian government's role and interest in the study of flying saucers.

I would like to thank James Smith, Wilbert Smith's son, for providing me with some new and interesting revelations about his father and his work, especially in light of anti-gravity experiments currently being conducted by the National Aeronautics and Space Administration (NASA). I would also like to thank Jack Litchfield, for allowing me to recount a most intriguing meeting he and a colleague had with Wilbert in 1954, as well as Ira Lewis and my editor, Jim Gifford. I am grateful to those who have sent me accounts of their sightings, and I would urge others to do so as well. In particular, I am interested in hearing from military personnel. I can be reached care of my publisher.

Palmiro Campagna
Orleans, Ontario, 1998

Preface

Do unidentified flying objects exist? Do they come from other planets? Or are all the reports nothing but hoaxes? And are all the files on the subject open, or is the government involved in a cover-up?

Answers to these and other perplexing questions are elusive, but in the following pages I have attempted to piece together the scenario that has evolved in Canada over the last fifty years. The information comes from several sources, including files I had declassified as recently as 1996 and even then only after I filed access requests, and from interviews with eyewitnesses and officials. The picture that emerges is sometimes confusing and often deceptive, with many riddles surrounding a few truths.

If one certainty has emerged in the research for this book, it is that things are not always what they seem. One must always keep an open mind. I have presented the facts as I found them and have offered my own speculation and thoughts in specific circumstances. In the end, though, it will be up to you the reader to decide whether or not to believe that this earth has or is being visited.

I am indebted to a number of people whose comments and advice I greatly appreciate. Some special individuals must be mentioned. As with my first book, on the Avro Arrow, I must acknowledge my wife, Jane, who again put up with my long hours at the archives and on the computer and who offered insight to the manuscript; Major Vern LaRue (retired), who provided information and comments to the manuscript; Captain Wolf Hassenklover (retired), for his experience in the Bermuda Triangle and Area 51; colleague and friend Roberto Brun Del Re, P. Eng., for encouraging me to begin the project; my brother Dr. Angelo Campagna, for getting me hooked on the whole subject back in 1966 with a copy of *Flying Saucers: Serious Business* by Frank Edwards; my parents, Paolina and the late Gilberto Campagna; my good friends Mark Smrdel and Mike Trushyk, for their encouragement; UFOlogist and early Canadian researcher Arthur Bray, for providing the Wilbert Smith material; the late Dr. Omond Solandt, former chairman of the Canadian Defence Research Board, for information provided in 1991 on Wilbert Smith and Dr. Vannevar Bush; Bob Oechsler, former NASA mission specialist, for information on the Guardian case; Colonel G. W. Patterson (retired); Owen Maynard, former chief, Systems Engineering Division, NASA; Mr. Murray Willer, P. Eng.; Major George A. Filer, USAF (retired); and Major W. March, from the Directorate of Air History in Winnipeg.

Finally, I would like to thank those at the National Archives in Ottawa, especially Paul Marsden; Glenn Wright at the RCMP archives in Ottawa; Laurie McKim at the National Defence

Headquarters library; the folks at Stoddart Publishing, namely Don Bastian, Stephen Quick, and Kevin Linder; Janet Rosenstock, for her insights to the manuscript; and former editor Mike Carroll, for early encouragement and work on the Arrow book.

Abbreviations

ADC	Air Defence Command (Canada)
AFOSI	Air Force Office of Special Investigations on Aerial Phenomena
APRO	Aerial Phenomena Research Organization
ATIC	Air Technical Intelligence Center
CAA	Civil Aviation Authority
CBC	Canadian Broadcasting Company
CFAO	Canadian Forces Administrative Order
CIA	Central Intelligence Agency
CIRVIS	Communications Instructions for Reporting Vital Intelligence Sightings
DAI	Director, Air Intelligence (Canada)
DMI	Director, Military Intelligence (Canada)
DND	Department of National Defence (Canada)

DNI	Director, Naval Intelligence (Canada)
DOD	Department of Defense (U.S.)
DRB	Defence Research Board (Canada)
DSI	Director, Scientific Intelligence (Canada)
GAO	General Accounting Office
JANAP	Joint Army Navy Air Force Publication
JCEC	Joint Communications Electronics Committee
JIC	Joint Intelligence Committee
NASP	National Aero-space Plane
NDOC	National Defence Operations Centre (Canada)
NEPA	Nuclear Energy for the Propulsion of Aircraft
NICAP	National Investigations Committee on Aerial Phenomena
NORAD	North American Air Defense Command (joint U.S./Canada)
NRC	National Research Council (Canada)
ONI	Office of Naval Intelligence (U.S.)
RAAF	Roswell Army Air Field
RCAF	Royal Canadian Air Force
RCMP	Royal Canadian Mounted Police
SAP	Special Access Program
USAF	United States Air Force

THE
UFO
FILES

One

Early Sightings

"Direct, convincing and unequivocal evidence of the truth of ETA [Extraterrestrial Actuality] would be the greatest single scientific discovery in the history of mankind."[1]

Edward U. Condon, <u>Scientific Study of Unidentified Flying Objects</u>, 1969

In the early 1970s, Corporal Wolf Hassenklover was an instrument electrical technician aboard a Canadian Argus coastal patrol aircraft. Designed to detect submarines, the Argus was loaded with sophisticated photographic and monitoring equipment. The aircraft and its crew had been part of a routine annual submarine-hunting exercise called Springboard, and were returning home from Bermuda to the Canadian Forces Base in Greenwood, Nova Scotia.

After a standard pre-flight check to ensure everything was ready, the aircraft took off on its flight home. It was early morning and the sky was clear with no clouds in sight. For a couple of hours it was a rather uneventful flight. Then suddenly, the compasses started going "crazy." At this point, the plane's radar picked up three unexplained blips, just before the voltage from the main generators dropped off. Both the radio and the radar went down. Finally, all power shut down save for the emergency battery backup. No one knew what was happening and Hassenklover could find no logical explanation. He checked and double-checked all the instruments and connections looking for the source of the problem. Then the radio operator signaled there was something out the window. Adding to the tension, the aircraft had entered the region of the infamous Bermuda Triangle.

Off the port wing, Hassenklover saw three lights, which he described as "brighter than Venus." The lights formed an "L" shape and followed the aircraft, all the while expanding and contracting their formation. They each had a different color: yellow, red, and white. The apparent shape was not recognizable as that of any known aircraft. Could they be planets distorted through some optical illusion? When the pilot banked the aircraft, the lights did likewise, staying off the port wing. As the aircraft turned, the lights followed, always maintaining position, demonstrating they belonged to some kind of craft or crafts under control.

Flying only on battery power was beginning to make the crew uneasy, especially as they had no radio to call for help should the situation develop into an emergency. After about ten minutes, just before the Argus reached the point of no return as its battery power drained, the lights took off at high speed in three separate directions, like a star burst. They disappeared as quickly as they had come. About fifteen seconds after their departure, main power in the Argus was restored. Whatever the problem had been, it was gone with the lights. The pilot immediately radioed the incident to the base at Greenwood, adding that photographs had been taken by the cameras on board.

The remainder of the flight was uneventful, until the aircraft arrived at home base. The military is well known for doing things "by the book." Procedures for everything are well defined in operational orders. Imagine then the surprise of the crew on landing when they found, waiting on the tarmac as the aircraft rolled to a stop not only the emergency vehicles which had responded to the original distress call, but military police. This was thought to be highly unusual and nonstandard practice. As the crew disembarked, another nonstandard practice was invoked: the military police took all the film canisters off the airplane.

This action prompts the following questions: Why were the military police called in to confiscate the film? Where did they end up taking the film? What did the film show? Does it still exist? Why the unusual procedures and secrecy?

This incident, along with the unanswered questions it raises, illustrates a conspiracy of silence that seems to surround certain well-documented UFO sightings. In the United States, where the focus of UFO research has understandably centered, there are many investigators and others who believe that the government has deliberately covered up and even distorted the facts about UFOs. Books such as the recently published *Top Secret/Majic* by Stanton Friedman demonstrate a growing awareness of the extent to which the American government has buried the truth and misled its own citizens.

North of the border, Canadians have inherited a similarly rich history of reported and unreported sightings covering every aspect of the UFO phenomenon. And as the above incident demonstrates, the reactions of the Canadian government and military have often been equally suggestive. Evidence has seemingly disappeared, while files that could often cast new light on both Canadian and American UFO sightings have been classified as top secret and tucked away for years, sometimes for decades. Canada, like the United States, seems to be hiding something — but what?

Those who do not believe in beings from outer space tend to dismiss the accusation of a "conspiracy of silence" among governments as being a product of the paranoid mind which distrusts government so thoroughly that conspiracies are seen everywhere. Some say that the sightings of UFOs are a byproduct of our scientific century, two World Wars which saw extraordinary development in space and aircraft science, and, of course, cold war fears. But how then to account for reportings of UFOs prior to this century?

In the UFO archival records in Ottawa, there is a curious letter from 1954. The author, a seventy-five-year-old Professor Bradley of Battleford, Saskatchewan, claims he was building toy models of disk-shaped objects in the 1890s as a child. He had his own sighting, which he described as "a mighty silver disk, darting up and down and which way, shedding little silver disks and a few red." The craft must have landed because he goes on to say, "I do not know where the men came from, but men like what I saw, well men like that are not born on earth."[2] Are these the ravings of a lunatic, or the words of a mischievous senior having some fun? The story may be a tall tale or, perhaps, a carryover from the mysterious airship sightings of the same period in the 1800s.

Between 1896 and 1897, at a time when dirigibles were not yet capable of sustained flight, hundreds of people across the United States and Canada reported seeing strange cigar-shaped objects in the sky. Some claimed they met with and spoke to the occupants of these craft. To this day, although some of the sightings have been deemed fabrications and hoaxes, there are those who believe that at least a few sightings were of either man-made experimental aircraft or, as Professor Bradley believed, not of this world. The following sightings are of interest if only because of their described similarity to modern sightings.

On August 12, 1896, a mysterious airship was seen over Rossland, British Columbia. It appeared as a luminous ball of fire as it approached the town. It could have been a meteor streaking across the sky, but then it "made seven wide circles, and then sped away on a straight course."[3] If it had been a meteor, it should have just kept going straight.

In 1897 a luminous, cigar-shaped object was sighted off Vancouver Island. It was traveling low in the sky and at times would flash a bright light. The incident was reported in the *San Francisco Chronicle* of August 13, 1897, under the title "Strange Visitors in Northern Skies."

Nineteen hundred and nine brought a wave of mysterious airship sightings over Britain and, oddly, New Zealand. Then, in 1911, there was an appearance over Chatham, Ontario. As reported in the *Windsor Record* of March 7, 1911:

Last night it was seen by parties in Chatham Township when it was brilliant with lights. For a time it floated along about 100 feet from the earth's surface, then suddenly with a great whirring, it rose to a high altitude and soon disappeared.[4]

Brilliance is a characteristic of most nighttime sightings, as are incredible speed and maneuvering. These attributes are apparent even in these early reports. And, it might be added, a "cigar shape" is entirely in keeping with the "thin edge of the wedge" so often reported.

A spectacular sighting and perhaps one of the best early documented, occurred the night of February 9, 1913. Eyewitnesses from central Canada and the U.S. reported that at 9:05 p.m. a fiery red object appeared in the northwestern part of the sky. As it got closer to the observers it seemed to get bigger, with a long tail trailing behind it. It was eventually reported by observers as far south as northeastern Brazil. At first, witnesses believed it was a large rocket. Unlike a rocket, though, it showed no sign of returning to earth. It simply continued on its relatively slow course until it disappeared from view.

Shortly after its disappearance in the distance, a stream of smaller objects, originating from the same point in the sky as the first, passed overhead. They were described as moving in formation, all at the same speed. They followed the same trajectory as the large object, disappearing at the same southeastern portion of the sky. A high school student in Trenton, Ontario, who saw the objects through opera glasses, estimated there were ten groups of objects consisting of twenty to forty smaller ones.

Professor C. A. Chant of the University of Toronto published requests for information of this sighting in various newspapers and received hundreds of reports in return. He analyzed each description and produced his findings in *The Journal of the Royal Astronomical Society of Canada*. Chant estimated the procession of objects, which he labeled as meteors, to have been in view for approximately three minutes. He calculated their speed between five and ten miles per second at an altitude of twenty-six miles. Under these circumstances, these were no ordinary meteors. Even if his calculations of height and speed were incorrect, the length of time they were in view across the continent was well beyond that of meteorite phenomena. Meteorites quickly burn up and extinguish. Meteorites also eventually hit the ground if they are not fully consumed in the atmosphere. These "meteorites" were not descending but rather, maintaining a constant altitude. A sound like thunder was also heard in the distance as the objects approached. In fact, three distinct sets of rumbling were heard, and Chant noted that in some communities buildings shook as the objects passed overhead.

The procession of objects was repeated five hours later, across the same path. This is an unusual event in itself when one considers that with the earth's rotation, the path of the objects across the sky should have been displaced. Whatever these objects were, it was as if they were orbiting with the planet, thereby maintaining their flight path in the sky. The following day, at approximately 2:00 p.m., office workers in Toronto reported seeing "dark objects moving out over the lake from west to east in three groups and then returning west in more scattered formation . . ."[5] Assuming the report to be legitimate, one is left to wonder if these objects were somehow related to the ones seen the night before.

Several theories were put forward to explain the event about which Dr. Chant wrote. Most of those theories dealt with some form of cosmic phenomenon such as meteors stacked one on top of each other, entering the atmosphere in pieces, giving the illusion of a procession. Other scientists believed there were several different events which, when taken as a whole, gave the impression of a procession following a singular path. None of these theories fit the observations, and the sightings remain unexplained to this day.

In reviewing the numerous letters he received in response to his newspaper request, Chant himself noted:

Many [witnesses] compared them to a fleet of airships, with lights on either side as well as forward and aft; but airmen will have to practice many years before they will be able to preserve such perfect order.[6]

Though Chant himself concluded these objects were some kind of meteor, his witnesses seemed to be describing craft under intelligent control.

Most reports estimated that between fifteen and twenty objects were involved but others noted as many as sixty or a hundred. Chant speculated that some witnesses may have been counting only the largest bodies, while others may simply have had better eyesight or better vantage points.

Another interesting facet of this incident is that the credibility and sobriety of the witnesses was never questioned. The possibility of the entire episode being a hoax was ruled out by the consistency of the reports and the sheer volume and diversity of the people involved. These truly were unidentified flying objects.

In 1914 an incident occurred where beings were reported as having been seen. William J. Kiehl was sixteen years old at the time. He was traveling out west with two others. The three teamed up with a French Canadian family who had a boat and were about to travel west along the north shore of Lake Ontario. Towards the end of the journey the boat developed a leak and the group set ashore.

Later in the day, at about 5:00 p.m., they noticed a strange craft sitting on the water. It looked like a globe with a flattened top. Two beings were standing on a deck-like structure manipulating a green hose that was in the water. They were about four feet in height and were wearing tight-fitting suits. The suits were green or purple depending on how the sunlight reflected off them. They had what looked like yellow boxes on their heads. Three others were seen at the top of the craft. The beings on the craft noticed Kiehl and his group watching. They got back into their craft and flew off. One did not quite make it back inside the craft and was still hanging on as the craft departed. Kiehl only made his account public in 1966. Although he was questioned at length about it, he stuck to his story.

The Kiehl incident is similar to another event, which took place in July 1950 and was reported in the *Steep Rock Echo*, the newspaper of the Steep Rock Iron Mines. In this instance, however, the story had been concocted as a joke by employee Gordon Edwards, according to the editor of the paper.

February 14, 1915, ended in the night of the "Phantom Invasion." It was 9:15 p.m. when lights were seen in the sky over Brockville, Ontario. They were over the St. Lawrence River and heading towards Ottawa. Coming from the direction of Morristown, New York, one of the objects was seen to drop three balls of fire or flares, which fell harmlessly into the water. The sound of a whirring motor could be heard as the objects passed. Sir Robert Borden, the Prime Minister of Canada, was notified that unidentified and potentially hostile aircraft were making their way to Ottawa. He in turn alerted the Chief of Staff of the Militia. The Commissioner of the Dominion Police was also advised. Fearing an invasion, the lights on Parliament Hill were turned off at 11:15 p.m. so that it would not be seen as a target. Shortly thereafter the city lights went out, and those of Rideau Hall and the Mint were also extinguished. Armed men were sent to the rooftops and orders were given to shoot down any invading aircraft.

The objects were later identified as balloons with fireworks attached. They had been sent aloft from Morristown, in celebration of the hundredth anniversary of the ending of the War of 1812. The following day, paper balloons were recovered in Brockville, which tended to corroborate the story but did not explain the whirring motor sound. Interestingly, people in Richmond Hill, north of Toronto, also reported a strange aircraft, and unusual lights were also seen further west in Guelph, over the agricultural college. Were these also part of the Morristown balloons? Three residents of Morden, Manitoba, reported an unusual "aeroplane" around the same time. This could not possibly have been the balloons. On February 19, some kind of aerial object was seen approaching from Lake Erie, passing over Buffalo and heading towards Canada. It was reported by thousands in the Buffalo area. Was this a delusion caused by mass hysteria? Was it an experimental aircraft? An extraterrestrial spacecraft? Or was it perhaps some other unknown phenomenon?

One other early incident is worthy of mention even though the connection to UFOs was only made years later. In fact, UFOs are not even mentioned in the account, which reads more like a description of the mysterious abandonment of the *Marie Celeste*.

On November 29, 1930, the Halifax *Herald* carried the sensational headline, "Tribe Lost in Barrens of North: Village of Dead Found by Wandering Trapper, Joe Labelle." It was written by Emmett E. Kelleher, in The Pas, Manitoba. Kelleher wrote that 500 miles northwest of the port of Churchill, Manitoba, a tribe of Eskimos (sic) had disappeared in the area known as Lake Angikuni. They left behind their dogs and tents. Joe Labelle, a trapper, had stumbled onto the area. In the account of what he witnessed, he stated:

> There were six tents made out of skin . . . I was a little jumpy . . . I expected to find corpses inside [the tents]. But there was nothing there but the personal belongings of a family . . . as if it had been left just that way by people who expected to come back . . . I figured there had been about 25 people in the camp, but all signs showed the place hadn't been lived in for nearly 12 months . . . I found the other tents in a similar state . . . I stayed around all afternoon, trying to figure things out. There were no signs of any struggle. Everything looked peaceful. But the air seemed deadly . . .[7]

The Royal Canadian Mounted Police investigated the story and found it to be without foundation. It was labeled a hoax and the file was closed. Sergeant Nelson, the investigating officer, wrote on January 5, 1931:

> In conversation with Mr. D. Simons, recently, who operates a trading post at Windy Lake, N.W.T., and has just returned from visiting his post by plane; he doubts the suggestion that any such calamity has occurred, as no doubt there would be reports from reliable white trappers and Eskimos of that district . . . Joe Labelle the trapper who is alleged to have related the story to Emmett E. Kelleher, the correspondent, is considered a new-comer in this country. The Manitoba records show this to be his first season, that he has taken out a trapping license, he is located on some of the lakes north of Flin Flon, and doubts are expressed as to whether he has ever been in the territories.[8]

Sergeant Nelson explained that the photograph accompanying the article had in fact been taken by a Mr. Rose, an ex-member of the Force, in 1909. He was stationed at Fort Churchill but was now living in The Pas. According to Rose, Kelleher had obtained the negative from him some time earlier and made a copy. He was now using that picture to back up his article on "The Village of the Dead."

Nelson said he believed the entire story was a work of fiction because Kelleher was apparently known for writing colorful pieces on the North and few people gave credence to his articles. Kelleher was out east at the time of Nelson's investigation and would be interviewed should he return to The Pas.

Dwight Whalen, writing in *Fate* magazine in November 1976, also concluded that the story was a hoax. He based his argument on the letter by Nelson. Whalen found no independent corroboration from other sources and chalked the whole thing up to "the story of an inexperienced trapper told to an imaginative and not too conscientious newsman."[9]

Perhaps the story was indeed a work of fiction, but several issues remain to be resolved, as Whalen himself pointed out. First, there is no record that Kelleher was subsequently interviewed by Nelson or anyone else. There is no record that he ever admitted the story was a hoax, unlike the case of the Steep Rock Iron Mines hoax. Kelleher's use of an old photograph for his illustration is no different than what newspapers and other news media do today with file pictures. In fact, sometimes photographs are staged to add something extra to a given story. This in itself does not render the story fictitious.

What about Joe Labelle? What did he stand to gain by telling such a story? More important, was he ever interviewed by the RCMP? The tone of Nelson's letter suggests that he was not. Instead, a man unconnected to the story (Simons) was interviewed and on the basis of his opinions and suppositions, the matter was closed.

That Labelle was a newcomer to the area sounds initially like a plausible explanation, but for what? Is the implication that newcomers are not to be trusted? If anything, one might expect it to have been an experienced oldtimer pulling a prank on his buddies. Did anyone check to see if Labelle had in fact been in the Angikuni area, and did anyone attempt to find the location of the alleged village? Until these questions are satisfactorily answered, it would seem that the story of "The Village of the Dead" may yet have some life.

Fact or fiction, this story has since been linked with alien abduction cases. That no UFOs were reported is irrelevant. The story has become part of Canada's UFO scene.

A much more recent example of UFOs over Canada's North occurred in 1996. The January 22 and 29 issues of *News/North* reported sightings from the region south of Great Slave Lake. On several occasions, witnesses, including the mayor of Fort Resolution and an RCMP constable, saw a bright light, which would change in color from blue to red to green and white, while moving across the sky. Witnesses noted it would then disappear from view by shooting straight upward into the sky. In a few instances it was said that car engines failed while the object (or objects) was in sight.

The sightings were reported to, and investigated by, the Department of National Defence, which even analyzed film footage that had been taken by a witness. The film showed a light but, with no reference points, it was difficult to conclude anything, including whether the apparent motion of the object was real or due to the individual's movement while filming. Although the film was duly returned, rumors circulated that the military had confiscated it. The sightings themselves remain unexplained.

Two

The Canadian Connection

"Then the saucers do exist?"[1]

Wilbert B. Smith, September 15, 1950

From mysterious airships to lights over the Bermuda Triangle to UFOs in the Far North, strange objects in the skies have appeared to hundreds of Canadians through the years. Crop circles have been reported at a time when that phrase was not yet coined, and in 1967 a close encounter left permanent scars on the witness, Stefan Michalak. Perhaps some of the most startling revelations have come from the personal notes of one Wilbert Smith, a Canadian engineer who in 1950 became the confidant of a pre-eminent American scientist. Therein lies the tale of the Canadian connection.

Wilbert Brockhouse Smith was born in Lethbridge, Alberta, in

1910. In 1934 he received his Master of Science degree in electrical engineering from the University of British Columbia. In 1939, after having worked as chief engineer with the radio station CJOR in Vancouver, he joined the Canadian Department of Transport. In succeeding years he was made superintendent of radio regulations engineering. In this position his responsibilities included equipment standards, broadcast facilities, radio interference studies, and radio relay systems. Smith's position and stature at the Department of Transport allowed him to participate in international conferences and meet a host of scientific personalities. He was highly regarded and respected in his field, inside Canada and abroad.

In 1947 he was in charge of establishing a network of ionospheric measurement stations across Canada. In his studies of radio-wave propagation, he investigated the fields of cosmic radiation, atmospheric radioactivity, and geomagnetism. With respect to the last, his studies indicated that it might be possible to use and manipulate the earth's magnetic field as a propulsion method for vehicles. In his theoretical and laboratory work, Smith pursued this idea and actually built a small experimental model. When activated, the model appeared to levitate ever so slightly. He attempted to confirm this effect by weighing his model before and after it was turned on. However, it was later said that his measuring technique was in error, and therefore that his model was not levitating.

As the Canadian delegate to the North American Regional Broadcasting Conference, Smith traveled to Washington in 1950. While there, Smith came across two books that had just been published on the subject of unidentified flying objects, *The Flying Saucers Are Real*, by Major Donald Keyhoe (retired), and *Behind the Flying Saucers*, by reporter Frank Scully. Both books claimed that flying saucers were indeed from outer space.

Keyhoe also asserted that vital information on flying saucers was being withheld from the public by the U.S. government. Scully's book went even further, claiming that the U.S. government had in fact retrieved a crashed disk, and that preliminary analysis indicated it operated on some sort of geomagnetic principle.

Wilbert Smith was more intrigued by the idea of spacecraft operating on a geomagnetic principle than he was with aliens from outer space. Such a geomagnetic principle fit in with his own theories of manipulating the earth's magnetic field for propulsion. But what about Keyhoe's claim that the government was not telling all it knew? While in Washington, Smith did more than just read these two books on the subject of UFOs. He made his own inquiries, and later described his discoveries in a secret memo that has since become one of the most controversial documents ever to come to light on the subject of UFOs.

Before exploring Smith's revelations, however, some background on what was occurring with respect to UFOs and the U.S. government, in particular the U.S. military, is in order.

During the Second World War, American, British, and French pilots fighting in Europe reported that strange circular, glowing objects, often orange in color, would sometimes follow their aircraft. The objects were dubbed "Foo fighters." According to the pilots, they would approach allied aircraft, follow them for some time, then fly away. The incident below is typical.

Lieutenant Meirs' aircraft belonged to the U.S. 415th Night Fighter Squadron. Several objects were seen by the crew but the aircraft's radar showed no sign of other objects in the vicinity before it began to malfunction. The airmen satisfied themselves that they observed some form of experimental device sent aloft to confuse them or their radar.

On December 22, 1944, two other pilots from the 415th Squadron reported a similar event:

> At 0600 . . . near Hagenau, at 10,000 feet altitude, two very
> bright lights climbed toward us from the ground. They lev-
> elled off and stayed on the tail of our plane. They were huge
> bright orange lights. They stayed there for two minutes. On
> my tail all the time. They were under perfect control . . .[2]

As it turned out, the bulk of the Foo fighter sightings came from
the 415th. Explanations for the phenomena included massive hallucinations, a natural display of electricity known as Saint Elmo's
fire, balloons, and, of course, experimental radio-controlled Nazi
devices.

According to Renato Vesco's book, *Intercept UFO*, the Nazis
did in fact have a number of devices that could have accounted
for these sightings. He states:

> Project Feuerball was first constructed at the aeronautical
> establishment at Wiener Neustadt, with the help of the
> Flug-funk Forcschungsanstalt of Oberpfaffenhoffen (F.F.O.)
> . . . during the day it looked like a shining disk spinning on
> its axis and during the night it looked like a burning globe.[3]

Did the German factories have such devices under construction,
and if so, were they working on disks large enough to carry
troops and armaments? Rumors have persisted that the Germans
built flying saucers but that the developments occurred too late
in the German war effort to make a difference.

In 1959 the English translation of *German Secret Weapons of
the Second World War* appeared in print. In it, author Rudolf
Lusar, Major of the Reserve (retired), also claimed that the saucers
were of German design. He alleged that they were developed by
people such as Richard Miethe, Rudolf Schriever, and the Italian
Bellonzo. One model was allegedly test-flown on February 14,

1945, reaching an altitude of 12,400 meters (7.7 miles) and a speed of 2,000 km/h (1,240 mph) in horizontal flight. Lusar further claimed that the factory in Breslau where Miethe worked was overtaken by the Russians. As in other instances, all the material and some experts were supposedly taken to Siberia to continue their work on these craft. This could all have been merely postwar propaganda, but there might have been some truth behind the stories, as Vesco claimed.

In the files of the Defence Research Board, there is a report from the Central Intelligence Agency called "Information From Foreign Documents or Radio Broadcasts, Report #00-W-25291; Subject - Military - Unconventional Aircraft, 1953." This report details documents of UFO sightings from around the world, including Denmark and Israel. In this issue it says that Rudolf Schriever, a former pilot, after eleven years of research into flying saucer designs, applied for a patent in West Germany. The date: November 20, 1952.

In early June of 1952, according to archival records, an ex-RCAF officer informed Air Force Headquarters in Ottawa of a German immigrant named Oskar Spatz living in Cornwall, Ontario. Spatz claimed to have knowledge of German flying saucer design and production. Subsequently, Spatz was interviewed on three separate occasions, the first commencing on June 21, 1952. He explained that while attending a civilian flying school where he studied aeronautics and learned to fly, he was noticed by one Captain Muller, a German intelligence officer in charge of special projects. Spatz and eleven others were selected for aircraft studies, and during this period a flying saucer was designed. He further claimed that later, between 1944 and 1945, while he was involved in military service, the saucer developments continued. Saucers were being assembled and tested at Stettin and at an undisclosed underground location southeast of Munich. Spatz was eventually captured in 1945 by American forces, but not before the saucer plans were all destroyed and Muller himself was killed.

During his subsequent interrogations, Spatz claimed he was the designer of the saucers and produced various drawings and diagrams. At this point, scientists from the National Research Council were called in to determine the legitimacy of the claims. Their unanimous conclusion was that Spatz had no specialized knowledge of aeronautics and that "there was nothing new, technically or in design, in the plans produced or information heard from source . . ."[4] The scientists decided that Spatz was probably just trying to use the story as an opportunity to gain employment or perhaps get a free trip home to Germany under the guise of revealing the location of the underground facilities. No further interest was expressed in the Spatz story, and the case was closed.

In September 1952 RCAF Headquarters was once again approached on the subject of German flying saucers. This time it was by Rudolf Goy, allegedly a German aeronautical engineer. His letter, translated from German states in part:

> . . . I want only to warn you about believing that these objects are emitted by the stars or that they are weather phenomena . . . In 1944 I and a group of scientists and technicians worked on a flying vessel that resembled the "flying saucers." In order to be safe from aerial attacks and to be able to work undisturbed our group was transferred to Silesia. Our experiments were made with models . . . In 1945 all was over . . . there was built an experimental model of 3.6 meters [11.8 feet] wing span . . . results were astounding . . . I am taking the liberty of informing also the "Air-vice Commander" of the U.S.A. Air Force.[5]

A response to these claims was issued through the Defence Research Board in Ottawa. The DRB requested an interview but Goy wrote back explaining he did not have the funds to travel to Ottawa.

Goy emphasized in his letter that he was not seeking personal gain in any way. He was concerned that the technology was being exploited by other countries, whose officials had seized the relevant documents after the war. He urged the Canadian government to build these devices, lest Canada be left behind in the technology race.

From a technical perspective, Goy warned against building a piloted craft without experimenting with models first. He claimed that a pressurized cabin would eventually be required in which the crew chairs would need to be gyroscopically stabilized. The Germans, he said, were also considering craft with no windows. The crew would look at pictures transmitted to TV screens instead. (This is a most interesting statement, for in March 1996, NASA reported the successful testing of a windowless cockpit system set up in a Boeing 737. By watching a monitor, pilots successfully landed their airplane. The system was being tested for future application in high-speed aircraft.)

The German project was four months away from completion, according to Goy, when the team was captured, presumably by the Soviets. He personally had fallen into American hands and was questioned by them about the saucer designs.

Despite all this information, Goy was not subsequently brought in for a thorough interrogation by Canadian officials, in spite of the fact that the DRB wanted a more in-depth interview with him. Instead, a note on his letter contains the following evaluation by someone at headquarters:

[Goy] appears to be an emotionally unbalanced individual, with no scientific knowledge on the subject which he tries to make us believe he knows something about . . . It appears from his letter he has been already thoroughly interrogated by the Americans in Western Germany . . . it is considered advisable to drop the matter . . .[6]

This dismissal of Goy seems problematic on several points. That he was unstable could hardly have been judged without a thorough, personal interview. As for his technical knowledge, it seems German and British scientists were indeed researching aircraft with gyroscopically stabilized cabins, as discussed by Vesco in his book, and Goy's caution on testing with models and windowless cockpits were legitimate and forward-thinking.

Another of those who believed the stories of Nazi-designed flying saucers was John Frost, a British aeronautical engineer. He felt he could duplicate the German designs. Frost's story will be taken up in a subsequent chapter.

There is an interesting aspect to the claims of both Spatz and Goy, one which does not seem to have been carefully investigated. That is the geographical relationship between the UFO sightings during the Second World War and the locations of research facilities given by Spatz and Goy. The 415th Squadron, which reported the bulk of the wartime sightings, was overflying territory reasonably close to the area in which Spatz claimed to have worked. On the other hand, the developments described by Goy took place near where Lusar said the developments were taking place. Perhaps there really was something more than propaganda or personal gain behind the Spatz and especially the Goy accounts.

In 1943 a classified project was apparently set up in Britain to study the Foo fighter reports. Under Lieutenant General Massey, investigations were to be conducted into reports from American, British, and French pilots. The following reference to ongoing work in intelligence circles, to identify the source of the objects, appeared in the *Washington Star* on July 6, 1947:

> . . . it was reported that Intelligence officers have never obtained satisfactory explanations of reports of flying silver balls and disks over Nazi-occupied Europe in the winter of 1944-45 . . . some Foo fighters danced just off the Allied fighters' wing tips and played tag with them in power dives . . . One Foo fighter . . . chased Lt. Meirs of Chicago some twenty miles down the Rhine Valley, at 300 m.p.h. . . . Intelligence officers believed at that time that the balls might be radar-controlled objects sent up to foul ignition systems or baffle Allied radar networks . . .[7]

At this point it must be stressed that sightings of this sort did not begin during the Second World War, nor did they end with the war. But this is when the U.S. military seems to have become officially involved.

On June 24, 1947, there was the now-famous UFO sighting by Kenneth Arnold, an American businessman. He was flying his airplane near Mount Rainier, in Washington State, assisting in the search for a downed plane, when he noticed nine odd-looking aircraft in the distance. He reported that their motion was like that of a saucer skipping across water, and he later calculated they were traveling at over 1,200 mph, faster than any airplane of the day. His story was broadcast over the news services and the term "flying saucer" was born. U.S. authorities were at a loss to explain his report but Arnold was taken seriously by many since he had a fine reputation and was well known both in the business world and as a pilot.

Then, a short two weeks after Arnold's report, UFO headlines again covered the front pages. On July 8, 1947, the *Roswell Daily*

Record, a newspaper in the town of Roswell, New Mexico, screamed the following headline: "RAAF Captures Flying Saucer in Roswell Region. No Details of Flying Disks Are Revealed." The Roswell Army Air Field (RAAF) had stunned the media with news of a crashed, and recovered, flying saucer. The Roswell story was carried around the world and the entire incident has since created a storm of controversy concerning the reality of alien spacecraft and a government cover-up.

The Roswell case has been laid out in detail by Kevin Randle and Donald Schmitt in *The Truth About the UFO Crash at Roswell*. The authors interviewed countless witnesses who came forward after more than forty years of silence. The following summary of the essential facts is presented here in order to show how certain information from Canadian sources provides an interesting perspective on the Roswell incident.

According to Randle and Schmitt, the Roswell incident began during the first week of July 1947. Several independent witnesses saw a shiny light fall to the earth. The occurrence was also recorded in the logbook of the Franciscan Catholic nuns of Saint Mary's Hospital, who thought an airplane had come down. The next morning, rancher Mac Brazel, who had heard a loud explosion the night before, rode through a field and found a considerable amount of debris. It appeared to be metallic in composition but was unlike anything he had seen before. Although the pieces were quite light, he was unable to cut them with a knife or burn them.

Major Jesse A. Marcel, an air intelligence officer with the 509th Bomb Group, the first squadron to have nuclear weapons (including the one dropped on Hiroshima), was sent to investigate. Major Marcel collected several pieces of the material. He too described them as unlike anything he had ever seen before. They were very light and did not burn when a cigarette lighter was put to them. He noticed strange color markings or writing on some of the pieces. To this day his son vividly recalls the strange nature of the material, which his father showed him and allowed him to handle.

Roswell mortician Glenn Dennis reports receiving a phone call on the night of July 5 from the base mortuary officer asking about the number of small caskets he had in inventory and which the base might need. Dennis was also asked how to prepare bodies in such a way so as not to chemically alter the blood or tissue. Since his mortuary also operated the local ambulance service, Dennis was later called to pick up an injured airman and bring him to the base. On the base, Dennis saw some unusual looking wreckage but after inquiring if there had been a crash, was told no, there had not been one. He was also requested to leave the base immediately. Before leaving, he was threatened by a military officer and advised that for his own good he should never reveal information about anything he had seen.

Dennis also claims that just before his encounter with the military officer, he saw a female nurse who was an acquaintance. He asked her what had happened. She told him to get out. About a day later he contacted her again, and eventually she told him that alien bodies had been recovered from a crashed saucer and she had been asked to assist in the autopsy, and she gave Dennis a description of the alien body.

Dennis would remain silent for many years before finally coming forward with his story. Perhaps he feared the threats that had been made against him by the officer. It is now being widely acknowledged that such threats were made at the time against individuals and their families should they reveal what they knew.

Marcel was subsequently summoned to Fort Worth, Texas, for a meeting with Brigadier General Roger Ramey. In the general's office several pieces of the debris were displayed. Marcel has since stated that he went into another room with the general, in order to show him on a map where the debris had been found. When he went back into the first room, the original debris had been replaced with that from a weather balloon. Reporters were then called in to photograph Marcel with the so-called wreckage. Thus the weather balloon cover was born and the Roswell incident that had earlier made headlines was relegated to obscurity for more than thirty years.

In 1995 one of the most controversial news stories of the past decade came out of Britain. A British filmmaker had come into possession of a most unusual piece of black-and-white film, part of which was aired on August 28, 1995, in a television program titled "Alien Autopsy." Ostensibly footage of an autopsy performed on an extraterrestrial being, the film will prove to be either an elaborate hoax or one of the most important discoveries of the twentieth century.

The film was supposedly taken by an American military cameraman who had been assigned the task of recording the autopsy on beings recovered from the flying saucer crash site near Roswell, New Mexico, in July 1947. The cameraman alleged that after shooting the film he had some difficulty developing and processing it, so he held some canisters back instead of sending them to his superiors. It was this withheld film which forty-eight years later he sold to the British filmmaker who then revealed it to the world.

The portion of film that was aired shows a humanoid creature with six fingers and toes, an oversized head, and large, almond-shaped eyes covered by a black membrane. The face is similar to those described in modern UFO accounts, although the ears, nose, and mouth appear more prominent than commonly mentioned. The medical equipment used during the autopsy, including the telephone in the room itself and the overhanging microphone, have all been dated to the correct time period of 1947. Medical experts have said the doctors in the film appear to be authentic in their behavior and conduct of the autopsy. Unfortunately, the doctors cannot be identified as they are each wearing some kind of anti-contamination suit. A third person behind a glass window is wearing a surgical mask, and at least one other person appears in one of the segments.

Hollywood special-effects experts remain divided on the question of authenticity as judged by their own art. Some have said that *if* this is a hoax then it is the most impressive they have ever seen. Such experts claim they are unable to duplicate certain effects such as the oozing out of fluid as incisions are made and the uniformity of the wetness beneath the skin layers as they are peeled back. Others have said that it is in fact possible to achieve these effects, but that whoever did it was a real professional. It is worth noting that the cameraman's name has not yet been revealed. The film has been in the possession of a London film company called Merlin Productions, owned by a man named Ray Santilli who continues to stick to his story about how the film was obtained.

As impressive as the film is, its authenticity is rightfully being questioned by scientists and researchers in the field of UFOs, and numerous additional questions have been raised, the most important of which concerns the identity of the cameraman. Since the film was aired, three other photos of a reported alien have appeared, in the September 1996 issue of *Penthouse* magazine. The photos purport to show an alien with features more closely resembling those described by Glenn Dennis, including an alien hand with what appear to be four fingers, not six as depicted in the video. These photos have since been shown to be fake. One wonders how many more photos or films will turn up; but will they prove to be legitimate?

In the 1980s papers known as the "Majestic Twelve documents" were obtained by researchers in the United States. These documents provide details about flying saucer crashes, including the Roswell crash, and about autopsies and a group of twelve individuals given the task of studying the aliens' remains. The papers purport to be briefing documents originally prepared for then President-elect Dwight D. Eisenhower.

Initially deemed authentic by some, the papers were said years later to be fakes, partly due to what appear to be inherent flaws such as a mixture of military and civilian formats in the dates used, supposed errors concerning known events, and signatures which may have been forged. The reputations and credibility of the researchers who studied the Majestic Twelve documents and declared them authentic suffered as a result. For this reason the autopsy video and any other such evidence must be thoroughly scrutinized, but even then, as often happens with UFO research, a final assessment may prove elusive. For example, in his most recent book, *Top Secret/Majic*, nuclear physicist and UFO researcher Stanton Friedman reveals new information concerning the Majestic Twelve documents and their authenticity, ably refuting the allegations of hoax and forgery.

The United States Air Force continued its investigations into the UFO phenomenon. On September 23, 1947, General Nathan F. Twining, Commander of Air Material Command, concluded in a secret memorandum that:

a. The phenomenon reported is something real and not visionary or fictitious.

b. There are objects probably approximating the shape of a disk, of such appreciable size as to appear as large as man-made aircraft . . .[8]

General Twining further noted that there was a lack of physical evidence (reinforcing the Roswell balloon cover story?) and that the possibility could not be ruled out that these objects belonged to a foreign nation with advanced propulsion techniques.

On December 30, 1947, the USAF established Project Sign to collect and investigate reports of unidentified flying objects. Based on the type of information gathered, the feeling within Project Sign was that the objects were indeed extraterrestrial vehicles. In 1949, at the request of the director of Research and Development, Project Sign became officially known as Project Grudge, although it was also referred to as Project Saucer in the media. By March of 1952 it became the infamous Project Blue Book, headquartered at Wright-Patterson Air Force Base.

A report produced by Project Grudge in August 1949 concluded that flying saucers did not constitute a threat to the security of the United States. Moreover, the report stated that sightings were the result of misidentifications of known objects, mass hysteria, or war nerves, and hoaxes. This appears to have been a significant reversal in thinking, since Project Sign had previously identified UFOs as interplanetary vehicles. The Grudge report recommended that the study of such objects be reduced in scope. The public reaction to the conclusions reached was to suspect that an official cover-up was now afoot, just as Major Donald Keyhoe had said in his book. But was he right? Through his own investigations, Wilbert Smith seems to have found an answer.

On November 21, 1950, Smith wrote a secret memo which has since created a sensation in the field of UFOlogy. Writing to his controller of telecommunications at the Department of Transport, Smith reported that while in Washington:

I made discreet inquiries through the Canadian Embassy staff in Washington who were able to obtain for me the following information:

a. The matter [of UFOs] is the most highly classified subject in the United States Government, rating higher even than the H-bomb.
b. Flying saucers exist.
c. Their modus operandi is unknown but a concentrated effort to discover the modus operandi is being made by a small group headed by Doctor Vannevar Bush.
d. The entire matter is considered by the United States authorities to be of tremendous significance.[9]

Smith's report sharply contradicts the Project Grudge conclusions and lends weight to Keyhoe's argument about a cover-up. Unfortunately, the information was never passed on to Keyhoe. Smith's memorandum also said:

I was further informed that the United States' authorities are investigating along quite a number of lines which might possibly be related to the saucers such as mental phenomena and I gather they are not doing too well since they indicated that if Canada is doing anything at all in geomagnetics they would welcome a discussion with suitably accredited Canadians . . . Mr. Wright, Defence Research Board liaison officer at the Canadian Embassy in Washington, was extremely anxious for me to get in touch with Dr. Solandt, Chairman of the [Canadian] Defence Research Board, to discuss with him future investigations along the line of geomagnetic release . . . Doctor Solandt agreed that work on geomagnetic energy should go forward as rapidly as possible . . .[10]

Not only does Smith's information appear to prove the existence of a cover-up, it also suggests the U.S. was actively investigating UFO phenomena along a number of different lines. Moreover, the involvement of Dr. Vannevar Bush speaks to the high priority given the subject. It is worth noting here that Bush is also cited in the Majestic Twelve documents as having been the scientist in charge of the analysis operation of the crashed disks.

Dr. Vannevar Bush was an electrical engineer. He developed the differential analyzer, the first electronic analog computer. He had taught at Tufts University and at the Massachusetts Institute of Technology. In the 1920s he devised the network analyzer to simulate the performance of electrical networks and in the 1930s his work at MIT foreshadowed the electronic computers developed after the Second World War. In 1940 Bush was appointed director of the U.S. National Defense Research Committee and in 1941 he became head of the Office of Scientific Research and Development, which co-ordinated all research and development for the war effort. After the war Bush was made chairman of the Joint Research and Development Board of the National Military Establishment. He was also president of the Carnegie Institution. In the American vernacular, Bush was a "heavy hitter" who would not have been involved in an area of research considered frivolous.

Clearly, the matter of UFOs had not officially been judged to be nonsense. The ongoing investigations to ascertain the existence of flying saucers and their occupants, as well as to solve the mystery of their propulsion systems, were just what Scully had reported in his book.

The Smith memo further suggests that a number of Canadians were likely in the know, most notably Dr. Omond Solandt, chairman of the Canadian military's Defence Research Board and the Canadian equivalent to Bush. Solandt admitted to this author in

1991 that he often spoke at length with his good friend Dr. Vannevar Bush on the subject of UFOs, but maintained that Bush never revealed anything about retrieved disks or alien bodies. Solandt said he and Bush would speculate at length as to what the UFO phenomenon was all about without ever finding a satisfactory answer. Unfortunately, my conversation with Solandt leaves unresolved the question, who provided Smith with his information?

In the early 1980s Canadian UFO researcher Arthur Bray, in sorting through Wilbert Smith's personal papers, found what are believed to be the original notes of Smith's discreet inquiries at the Canadian Embassy in Washington. Smith had been in touch with Lieutenant Commander (Canadian Navy) James Stewart Bremner, the naval member of the Canadian Joint Staff Washington (CANAVUS). Bremner in turn had put Smith in contact with a leading American scientist.

Bremner had also been a member of the Defence Research Board, before retiring from the forces in 1954. His own background is somewhat obscure. It seems that in the forties he had worked at the National Research Council in Canada, before being posted to the Canadian Embassy in Washington. Working at the embassy, Bremner was seemingly able to identify American scientists involved in UFO matters — but how?

On July 6, 1951, Bremner advised the embassy staff in Washington that the United States would complete their prototype "atomic powered aircraft"[11] within the year. His source was Rear Admiral J. Tate (retired). Admiral Tate had been in charge of the Naval Air Station in Olathe, Kansas.

The idea of a nuclear-powered aircraft was suggested right after the war. At that time the USAF began a project called Nuclear Energy for the Propulsion of Aircraft, or NEPA. From the onset there was controversy over the potential hazard, and as the difficulties and complexities became more evident, enthusiasm waned. Ten years later, when the hazards of nuclear power were even more evident and the expense of development more obvious on a risk/benefit basis, the project was supposedly abandoned. Bremner's reference appears to be the earliest foreign indication that the U.S. was developing an atomic-powered aircraft to the point of having a prototype ready, as opposed to merely investigating the possibility of nuclear power for aircraft propulsion. What type of aircraft was it? Could it have been related to the flying saucers? If so, perhaps Tate was the one who told Bremner about the scientists involved in UFO research.

The scientist who Bremner put Smith in touch with was Dr. Robert I. Sarbacher. At the time Sarbacher was, among other things, dean of Georgia Tech's postgraduate school and a consultant with the American Research and Development Board. According to Smith's notes, dated September 15, 1950, Sarbacher was the one who made the revelations concerning the flying saucers:

Smith: I have read Scully's book on the saucers and would like to know how much of it is true.
Sarbacher: The facts reported in the book are substantially correct.
Smith: Then the saucers do exist?
Sarbacher: Yes, they exist.[12]

Smith asked Sarbacher whether the saucers worked on geomagnetic principles, since this was what Smith was working on and it was what Scully had reported. Sarbacher said the method of propulsion had not yet been figured out but that the whole subject was classified "two points higher than the H-bomb."[13] When Smith asked how he could get more information, Sarbacher replied:

I suppose you could be cleared through your own Defense Department and I am pretty sure arrangements could be made to exchange information. If you have anything to contribute, we would be glad to talk it over, but I can't give you any more at the present time.[14]

This invitation by Sarbacher must be what led Smith to say in his memo to the Department of Transport's controller that the U.S. was willing to discuss geomagnetic propulsion research possibilities with accredited Canadians. It may also have been the impetus for Solandt to agree so readily to supporting a research effort led by Smith.

A logical question to ask at this point is why, if the matter was so highly classified, was Dr. Sarbacher saying anything at all about this work, and to a civilian rather than to Bremner or some other military person? It may be that Smith had already been checked out and cleared. With his high scientific profile, his work in geomagnetic propulsion theory, and the credibility he had established for himself in international scientific circles, he was seen as a good contact to whom some information could be revealed. If Sarbacher was sure an exchange of information could be established, that would indicate that the Canadian Department of National Defence was also in the picture, most likely through Bremner. And if Bremner knew, one can assume Solandt knew. Solandt would presumably have discussed the matter with Bush, his friend and the scientist in charge of the study of the crashed disks. In this way, Bush could have benefited from Smith's findings.

Was Smith's meeting with Sarbacher legitimate? According to William Steinman, author of *UFO Crash at Aztec*, it most certainly was. After researcher Arthur Bray released the Smith notes, Steinman was one of many to contact Sarbacher and query him on the meeting he had had with Smith back in 1950. In December 1983 Steinman received a letter, dated November 29, from Sarbacher, in which he confirmed his meeting with Smith in 1950 and reaffirmed what he had told Smith about the existence of the retrieved saucers. Sarbacher again stated that Dr. Vannevar Bush was definitely involved in the subsequent scientific analysis of the saucers, with special emphasis on how they were constructed and functioned, and that John Von Neumann, another prominent scientist, was also likely involved. Sarbacher also indicated that there was more than one saucer and thought Dr. Robert Oppenheimer, the man behind the atomic bomb, was also part of Bush's scientific team.

Unfortunately, Sarbacher said he personally had not taken part in any analysis, nor did he have any firsthand knowledge from seeing wreckage or bodies. He had been asked to participate in examining the saucers, but due to other commitments could not get involved.

In May 1985 Sarbacher was approached by Barry Greenwood, editor of a publication called *Just Cause*. In a telephone conversation with Greenwood, Sarbacher was again asked about the meeting with Smith. Sarbacher said his letter to Steinman was not a hoax and that the contents as far as he was concerned were true. He further stated that at the time of the saucer investigations, he was involved with the Research and Development Board (of which Bush was chairman), as chairman of the Guidance and Control Panel of the Guided Missile Committee. It was from others in the Research and Development Board that he had heard the stories of the crashed disks and the ongoing research in which he had been asked to take part. His colleagues had told him that the origin of all the information about the disks was at Wright Field at Wright-Patterson AFB.

Stanton Friedman spoke face to face with Sarbacher and

obtained similar information. In his book *Crash at Corona*, Friedman states that in 1985 Sarbacher told another researcher, Dr. Bruce Maccabee, that he had had an opportunity to go and see the recovered material. Sarbacher was unable to attend but colleagues who did go advised him that the alien bodies were insect-like or robot-like. It is most unfortunate that again Sarbacher had been unable to see the wreckage or bodies firsthand. Despite his impressive background, without firsthand corroboration his information, while startling, remains unsubstantiated. Also unfortunate is that no one seems to have asked which of his colleagues at the Research and Development Board were involved.

Sarbacher died in 1986, leaving all to wonder whether his whole story in 1950 was a concoction or his revelations were truthful. One thing is certain, Smith believed Sarbacher's claims completely, and whether Solandt believed them or not, he certainly urged Smith to move forward with his own research.

Three

The New Science

"It appears then, that we are faced with a substantial probability of the real existence of extra-terrestrial vehicles, regardless of whether or not they fit into our scheme of things."

Wilbert B. Smith

Wilbert Smith's request for research into geomagnetic energy and hence the potential discovery of UFO propulsion was sanctioned by both the Deputy Minister of Transport for Air Services, Commander C. P. Edwards, and the Assistant Minister, J. R. Baldwin, and on November 21, 1950, Smith took charge of a newly created project dubbed Project Magnet. Its original purpose was to study geomagnetic phenomena. The work was broken down into theoretical and laboratory studies of geomagnetics. The latter would include various investigations into the effects of magnetic fields on rotating, circular, metallic objects — such as propulsion systems for flying saucers.

Due to personnel problems in Smith's Broadcast and Measurement Section of the Department of Transport, the theoretical and laboratory work on geomagnetics had to be curtailed. Accordingly, "the only productive work which the group felt they could carry on was a detailed study of the sightings themselves."[1]

On January 3, 1951, Smith wrote to Gordon E. Cox, Third Secretary at the Canadian Embassy in Washington. Cox, along with James Bremner and Arnold Wright, had been one of the individuals who had helped orchestrate Smith's meeting with Dr. Sarbacher. Smith's purpose in contacting Cox was to bring the embassy staff up to date on Project Magnet. Smith said that three engineers and two technicians were working full-time with him and that the Canadian Defence Research Board was providing assistance wherever it could.

The project had become official and was designated secret. Smith noted that Dr. Solandt of the Canadian Defence Research Board had asked that the security classifications established by the United States be fully respected. This disproves statements in *UFO: The Government Files* by Peter Brookesmith, which contends that Smith had arbitrarily made up his security classifications. In the letter, Smith then asked Cox if he knew whether Solandt had obtained any additional information on the subject of UFOs from his most recent trip to Washington. Smith also broached the subject of Major Donald Keyhoe, with whom he had been in touch.

Smith had contacted Keyhoe shortly after reading his book in 1950 and discussed several issues with him, including the proposed magnetic propulsion mechanisms of the flying saucers. In their subsequent discussions Smith never revealed his meeting with Sarbacher. Based partly on some of these discussions with

Smith, Keyhoe wrote a draft article on UFOs which he was hoping to publish. Perhaps in an attempt to verify or legitimize Smith's information, Keyhoe had passed this article on to Solandt for review. Solandt had in turn given it to Smith for comment. Smith reviewed and redrafted Keyhoe's article to bring it more in line with the known facts and some reasonable speculation. Presumably, this meant postulating further the extraterrestrial origins of the saucers, without revealing the information obtained from Sarbacher.

Smith returned the article to Solandt, who returned it to Keyhoe via Wright, the Defence Research Board member at the Canadian Embassy mentioned in Smith's secret memo to the Department of Transport's controller. Keyhoe was asked to run the article past Dr. Vannevar Bush for final clearance for publication. In his letter to Cox, Smith expressed a desire to find out how Bush reacted to the article's revelations. Smith may have been concerned that he had revealed too much in the article and was anxious to find out if Bush's reaction would be negative. As far as can be determined, the article was never published by Keyhoe, although elements appeared in his later books. The entire affair, however, undoubtedly exposed Smith as a liability to the U.S. government, since he had been specifically asked by Solandt to keep matters quiet and respect their confidentiality.

Cox replied to Smith on January 6, 1951. Commenting on the UFO issue, Cox said there was nothing new to add:

> The official position is still that nobody knows anything about the matter here at all. We are, of course, keeping our ears and eyes open and if anything does develop you will probably hear through the Wright and Solandt channel. On the Ambassador's instructions no one in the Embassy, apart from Wright and myself, is to discuss the matter with anyone.[2]

With respect to Keyhoe's article, Cox replied that he had no knowledge of any reaction from Bush, and stated that if Smith was going to meet Keyhoe or obtain information from him, Cox would arrange it through Bremner.

Cox closed with this final observation:

The Ambassador and I would be particularly interested in any indication you may have heard when you were here on the possibility of an official U.S. Government statement. It is this political angle [with] which I will be principally concerned.[3]

Wright, Cox, and the Canadian Ambassador, Hume Wrong, were all aware of Smith's revelations, but they took the official line and pleaded ignorance of the whole matter. It was obviously a matter of great importance, since it had reached the Ambassador himself and was monitored by Cox for possible political ramifications. Did Wrong make further inquiries to the U.S government, either directly or through the Wright/Solandt channel? A search of the Canadian Ambassador's papers has turned up nothing thus far, and virtually no records appear to exist from Cox, Wright, or Bremner.

One can only wonder how Bush reacted to Smith's article. Did he discuss its contents with Solandt? Did he tell Solandt he was in charge of a scientific team to study the saucers? It seems plausible that he would have done so, but again no records to this effect have yet been found and Solandt himself denied it. Still, there are hints contained in other sources.

In June 1952 Smith issued an interim report for Project Magnet in which he wrote that from the limited information he had so far gathered on UFOs, it was difficult to deduce their operating characteristics. In particular, he was not able to establish whether they operated on geomagnetic principles. He further stated that due to the lack of actual pieces to examine, a direct approach to solving the puzzle was not possible. He did however indicate that other information had established their reality. Undoubtedly, Smith was referring to the information from Sarbacher, without actually mentioning their meeting two years earlier.

As part of his interim report, Smith included a description of a typical saucer, as derived from the reports he was able to analyze. The saucers were generally reported as thin and round, with a hemispherical bulge on one side. They were anywhere from 100 to 200 feet in diameter and about 10 feet thick in the center. They were metallic in appearance and highly reflective. Notably, their speed capability was reported as being extremely high, possibly as much as 18,000 miles an hour. Their power source was unknown but Smith did not believe they were chemically or atomic powered, possibly due to the absence of residues such as radioactivity. Generally they were reported as being silent except for a slight swishing sound. He noted that they could allegedly cause a compass needle to fluctuate, even from as far away as 10 miles (an effect also reported by aircraft and ships entering the Bermuda Triangle).

Then Smith had his own sighting. While driving along Wellington Street in Ottawa, he observed a UFO. Traffic had momentarily stopped, when something caught his eye. The disk he saw was a bright colored, silver, elliptical-shaped object. He estimated that it was 40 miles up and traveling at 9,000 miles an hour, and he judged its diameter to be 125 feet. His sighting fit the general description he had developed.

By August 10, 1953, Smith had produced a refined and final report on Project Magnet. He again noted that the characteristics of the objects seemed to rule out conventional methods of propulsion and that their behavior was beyond the capability of known earthly technology. Smith went on to stress that there was no scientific basis to believe they were optical illusions. He came to the following conclusion:

> It appears then, that we are faced with a substantial probability of the real existence of extra-terrestrial vehicles, regardless of whether or not they fit into our scheme of things. Such vehicles of necessity must use technology considerably in advance of what we have . . .[4]

There appears to have been no immediate official reaction to Smith's Project Magnet report, either from his own Department of Transport or from Solandt at the Canadian Defence Research Board; the report was neither endorsed nor rejected. Evidence that it was indeed submitted to the DRB is contained in a memorandum dated September 15, 1969, which stated that those wishing to see a copy of the Magnet final report would have to make an appointment with Dr. Peter Millman of the Canadian National Research Council. How Millman obtained a copy and his involvement in the whole affair will be explored later. For now, suffice to say that Millman had been recruited by Solandt to assist in the study of the UFOs.

Although Solandt remained silent on Smith's report, he must have felt there was merit in what Smith was doing, for on November 12, 1953, the following telegram was issued to the world news services:

> In a few weeks an observatory which, it is hoped, will elucidate the mystery of the flying saucers, will begin its work at Shirley's Bay, about twelve miles from Ottawa . . . directed by Mr. Wilbert Smith . . . Smith has made the following statement: "The odds are sixty to a hundred that they [flying saucers] are extra-terrestrial vehicles."[5]

Solandt, through the DRB, had provided Smith with the building he was going to use for his research station. The leak of this news about the station violated Solandt's request for secrecy. Smith had talked to the press and to Keyhoe again about work which was to have remained quiet. At the time, when asked, Solandt denied any knowledge of the existence of the research station.

As a scientist, Smith was hoping to obtain hard data which would provide some insight into the mode of operation and propulsion of the saucers. He stocked his research station with equipment from another project which had been discontinued, as well as some instruments made up in his laboratory or borrowed from the University of Toronto. His plan was to measure for anomalous electrical, magnetic, or radioactive disturbances which might indicate the presence of an alien vehicle. But first, because of the contents of the press release, he was compelled to write a memorandum to his department's controller of telecommunications, explaining how the press had found out.

Smith wrote in his memo that with the exception of a few highly significant sightings which remained classified, the security classification in the United States had been downgraded considerably. He pointed out that his own theoretical work on the subject had been discussed openly in scientific circles and that the exchange with other scientists had been beneficial. Finally, he noted that the press had learned of the existence of his work through a book called *Flying Saucers from Outer Space* by Major Keyhoe, with whom he had discussed his research plans.

Smith added in his memo that he had been inundated by the press since the publication of Keyhoe's book, and felt it best to answer questions with the facts, to avoid any wild speculation. He told reporters that the project was using reclaimed equipment, with no significant amount of funding. He ended his memo by stating his belief that the public was aware of the high probability that the saucers were alien in origin and that a concerted effort was required to exploit their technology. Smith was allowed to continue his work.

On April 27, 1954, the controller of telecommunications was sent another memorandum, this time from C. M. Brant, the superintendent of radio regulations. He had reviewed the work of Project Magnet in light of increasing workloads and staff shortages in the radio regulations subdivision. He wrote that the only analysis undertaken had been by Wilbert Smith and not by the Defence Research Board. As a result, "the Department has become involved in publicity related to 'flying saucers'"[6] — a fact about which Brant clearly seemed upset. In fact, other memos on file speak of the embarrassment that the publicity surrounding Smith's work was causing the Department of Transport. Brant was not interested in publicity and felt the DRB should take on the responsibility of studying UFOs. He therefore recommended the discontinuation of Project Magnet.

On June 10, Smith replied to Brant:

I am satisfied that there is a sufficient probability for the real existence of some Unidentified Flying Objects as Alien Vehicles, to warrant carrying on with the investigations and if possible, expanding them to include a more intensive study of the physics of the problem.[7]

Smith told Brant he would continue the work regardless, on his own, but outlined several possibilities for re-establishing the project elsewhere in his Department as he agreed it did not properly fall under the purview of the telecommunications division. Brant wrote on the memo that he was not in agreement with Smith's statement concerning the real existence of the saucers and sent the annotated memo to the controller of telecommunications asking for advice.

The controller, Mr. G. C. W. Browne, replied on June 25. He said the Assistant Minister of Transport had raised the matter with Solandt, who was of the opinion that no particular facts had come forward which warranted turning the study of UFOs into a special government project. Solandt said he had checked with his sources in the United Kingdom and in the United States and found that no special work was ongoing. No mention was made of the group under Bush. And what about the significant and highly classified sightings Smith had talked about? What about Project Blue Book, and what about Smith's own memo of 1950 and what Bremner knew?

Solandt further added that he and his personnel, given what they knew of what was happening in Washington, did not feel the need to add any more top-level individuals to the investigations and research as Smith had wanted. Solandt's statement was carefully worded, implying that top-level scientists were already involved, namely Vannevar Bush. It was agreed that Smith should be told to continue on his own if he so desired, with no official backing. While there was no objection to allowing Smith to continue using equipment not required elsewhere, the Department should, especially in the event of publicity, take the position that "there was no official Departmental sponsorship of Smith's activities."[8] Brant advised Smith accordingly on June 28.

Interestingly, at no time did Solandt dismiss Smith's conclusions. He could not if he too was aware of the information from Sarbacher and the involvement of Bush. All Solandt indicated was that no further work was necessary in Canada. Perhaps he was upset by the fact that Smith had gone to the media once too often, and was now trying to distance himself from him. Smith was now a liability. It is unfortunate that there is no record of what Solandt thought of Smith's conclusions or if he was even asked by the Assistant Minister.

In June 1991 Solandt told this author that there was no hard evidence of the existence of flying saucers but that Smith was allowed to continue his work because the DRB was keeping an open mind. This work, Solandt added, included the construction of a device which, when activated, gave the appearance of levitating. On closer scrutiny, the levitation was apparently due to measurement error, according to Solandt.

On August 8, 1954, at 3:01 p.m., Smith's equipment registered an anomalous disturbance. Unfortunately the sky was cloudy, and no visual observation of what was causing the reaction to the equipment could be made. News of the event was made public on August 9.

On August 10, obviously unhappy with the renewed publicity, Brant told Smith in writing to close down the research station in Shirley's Bay and return all the borrowed equipment.

News of the registration of an anomalous disturbance on Smith's equipment should have provoked renewed interest. Instead the Department appeared more concerned with public image and publicity. Presumably, as long as nothing was discovered, it was all right to allow Smith to continue with the work. But with possible tangible evidence at hand, the preferred course of action was to close Smith down.

Had the Department of Transport initiated a cover-up? Based on the material made available to me, it does not seem likely that Brant was trying to conceal anything. Brant's memos come across as being written by a man who quite simply did not believe in the existence of flying saucers and therefore genuinely felt that any publicity on the subject would be an embarrassment. Other correspondence on file indicates the same feeling.

For their part, the media were not all that kind to Wilbert Smith and his work. *Time* magazine, for example, spoke of Smith and his flying "crockery." Perhaps if the skies had not been cloudy that day, and if a few good photographs had been taken, the results might have changed Brant's mind and impressed the media — but such was not the case. Under the circumstances, Brant just did not want anything more to do with flying saucers.

Smith continued working on the project in his spare time, and in 1955 he reported to a House of Commons Special Committee on Broadcasting that there were no results from his UFO measurements.

By 1959 Smith had become involved with the U.S. Office of Naval Intelligence (ONI) and the Central Intelligence Agency (CIA). The latter had requested he participate in investigations in which "contact" through telepathic means was supposedly established with alien beings through a medium by the name of Mrs. Swan, but this activity was not entirely new. Smith's 1950 secret memo to the controller of telecommunications had mentioned that the Americans were investigating along a number of lines, including mental phenomena, and now Smith himself had become a participant. Smith continued working through Mrs. Swan in the ensuing years and referred to the aliens he spoke to through her as "the boys from Topside." The alien with whom he spoke most often was named AFFA. AFFA told Smith about new concepts of space and time, matter and energy, which Smith subsequently expounded upon in a manuscript he called *The New Science*.

Smith was so certain of the existence of extraterrestrials that one might wonder if on one of his many trips to the U.S. he was allowed to actually see a retrieved disk or the alleged bodies. Was Smith later truly in contact with superior beings? There are, of course, other explanations, as we shall see.

F●ur

Yes We Do, No We Don't

". . . in so far as the press and public were concerned at least, [the saucer studies] had been discontinued. Very recently, however, this investigation was re-opened, but is now classified."
Department of National Defence memorandum

Solandt insisted he never knew anything about crashed saucers, Vannevar Bush's involvement, or any of the other aspects of the mystery of the saucers revealed by Sarbacher. As it was, the report issued by Project Saucer (Grudge) had publicly denounced the subject. Yet Canada's Minister of National Defence took it all to heart.

In the papers of the Honourable Brooke Claxton, the Canadian Defence Minister in 1950, it is noted that he and Solandt met with Bush in 1948. It seems that Claxton was a particular fan of Bush's, having read some of his works. What transpired in the ensuing years is quite interesting.

In April 1950, well before Smith's meeting with Sarbacher, Claxton requested that Solandt obtain the co-operation of the three Canadian military services — army, navy, and air force — in reporting occurrences of flying saucers seen over Canada. Claxton suggested that the matter be discussed at a meeting of the Joint Intelligence Committee (JIC). This committee included representation from the Director of Air Intelligence (DAI), the Director of Naval Intelligence (DNI), the Director of Military Intelligence (DMI), and the Director of Scientific Intelligence (DSI).

The committee did discuss the matter, and the departmental records of this event state:

U.S. "Project Saucer" was completed about 1950 and it was found desirable to solicit Canadian reports. At the 220th meeting of the Joint Intelligence Committee, on the 12 April 1950, UFOs were discussed and the following decisions were reached:

(a) The Director of Scientific Intelligence and Director of Air Intelligence were to collaborate in preparing a questionnaire to be distributed to field intelligence officers of the three services and the RCMP.

(b) Director Air Intelligence is to co-ordinate the investigation arrangements in the field.

(c) All field reports were to be passed to the Director of Scientific Intelligence for official examination on behalf of the Department of National Defense.[1]

On June 29, 1950, a letter was sent from the Director of Air Intelligence to the Director of Scientific Intelligence. In it the DAI noted that a Canadian officer had been dispatched to Washington to learn more about the United States Air Force conclusions regarding Project Saucer. The officer came back recommending that the matter be quietly dropped; there was nothing to the UFO stories. The DAI's letter was followed by another, this time to the Joint Intelligence Committee, on August 4. This second letter further recommended that a questionnaire for investigating sightings not be developed, noting that a questionnaire was not required if the UFO matter was going to be dropped since the Americans had publicly stated that there was nothing to investigate. There is no mention of Bremner in this correspondence.

Despite these recommendations, the JIC did not drop the matter and a questionnaire was indeed drawn up, approved, and sent to field units with reporting instructions, under cover of document file "S21-1-9 (DAI) 19 October, 1950." The "S" in the document file indicates that it was classified "Secret." The number following the "S" is the numerical file number. DAI in brackets means that the covering letter was drafted by the Director of Air Intelligence in spite of his earlier recommendations to drop the subject.

It seems that someone in the Joint Intelligence Committee, or the Minister himself, knew something more about what was going on behind the scenes in Project Saucer. Why else would Claxton order the JIC to act despite the Project Saucer report which had publicly concluded there was nothing to the phenomena? Unless of course there was one conclusion for public consumption and a very different one for internal use, as Keyhoe had surmised. This would explain why the DAI's recommendation to drop the study of UFOs was overruled.

A search for the document of October 19 with the questionnaire has not yet proven successful. Also, there is no clear indication of how many UFO cases were subsequently reported or investigated, but there is evidence of an attempt to keep the matter quiet. Reflecting back on these events, a letter written to the Assistant Chief of the Air Staff (ACAS) in 1957 states: "There has been a recorded instance of October, 1950 . . . that reports would be filed, but investigations would be played down. There has never been an investigation of any report on file at AFHQ."[2]

The last statement is somewhat peculiar, especially given that the minutes of that JIC meeting state that one of the purposes of the questionnaire was to assist field intelligence officers and the Royal Canadian Mounted Police in their investigations.

Smith's Project Magnet and this questionnaire from the Joint Intelligence Committee notwithstanding, in 1952 the Department of National Defence formally organized a group to collect and analyze UFO sightings. Like the Americans with their Project Sign, Project Grudge, and Project Saucer, the Canadian group chose a code name which was perhaps too appropriate: Project Second Storey.

The first meeting of the Project Second Storey committee was held on April 22, 1952, chaired by Solandt. The secretary of the group was Mr. H. C. Oatway. Others in attendance included Squadron Leader L. P. S. Bing from the Joint Intelligence Service, Group Captain D. M. Edwards from the Directorate of Air Intelligence, Commodore J. C. Pratt from the Directorate of Naval Intelligence, Lieutenant Colonel E. H. Webb from the Directorate of Military Operations and Planning, Flight Lieutenant V. L. Bradley (DRB), Mr. A. J. Langley (DRB), Dr. Peter Millman from the Dominion Observatory, and of course, Wilbert B. Smith from the Department of Transport. Over succeeding meetings some names would change.

At this first meeting Solandt noted that based on the frequency of occurrence and persistent nature of the UFO phenomena, the idea that these were hallucinations should be ruled out. The committee also decided that the current approach to collecting and studying reports was haphazard and that a more structured method was desirable. The Second Storey meetings were intended to confirm if a more intensive effort was required in investigating the phenomena, and if so, to develop ways and means of organizing such an effort. The air force representative indicated that in the United States, work done in studying UFO reports by the USAF had resulted in little information of significance. But then he added:

> . . . in so far as the press and public were concerned at least, [the saucer studies] had been discontinued. Very recently, however, this investigation was re-opened, but is now classified.[3]

This comment was most likely made in reference to the findings of Project Grudge and its subsequent transformation into Project Blue Book in March 1952. It seems that the public was being given one conclusion, that is, that there was nothing to the phenomena and that studies into UFOs were being terminated, while in reality Project Blue Book was being initiated to study the UFOs as a classified effort.

According to Blue Book, the earlier conclusions from the Project Saucer (Grudge) report, which stated that UFO sightings were the result of hysteria and the like, had been overturned because reports were continuing and many were from reliable military personnel themselves. The reason given for the "Secret" security classification was to protect the names of those filing reports. As well, it was explained that the original classification of "Top Secret" had been used in earlier studies because no one knew where the investigations would lead. Now the classification had been downgraded to Secret, in the event that sensitive locations or classified equipment entered the discussion. No mention was made of crashed saucers, and it may be that this information, if real, was being held back even from Blue Book. One thing is certain, though, as pointed out by Stanton Friedman in *Top Secret/Majic*. Even Blue Book produced a report called "Special Report 14," which listed more than 600 unexplained sightings. However, the USAF publicly provided a diluted version of the report without giving its name or many of the startling facts it contained. The CIA was also convening a group to study UFOs. It was known as the Robertson Panel, since it was chaired by physicist Dr. H. P. Robertson. As Timothy Good points out in *Above Top Secret*, this panel seems to have been established to debunk sightings and discredit witnesses while concealing the truth.

At the Second Storey meeting, Smith took the opportunity to expound an extraterrestrial hypothesis. He had found an apparent correlation between the onset of sightings and the position of the planet Mars. He said the number of sightings increased when, due to their respective orbits, Mars and Earth came closer together in space. Smith then spoke about his own work with the Department of Transport's ionospheric stations. He indicated that no anomalous electromagnetic phenomena had been detected at these stations which might indicate the presence of a flying saucer. At no time during the meeting did Smith reveal his discussions with Sarbacher.

Oatway, the secretary of the group, told this author in 1995 that he was unaware of any discussions Smith had shared with Sarbacher. Oatway felt that Smith was a brilliant engineer in his field, but did not share his belief in extraterrestrials. If Solandt was aware of the information from Sarbacher, he too did not let on. It is important to note that everything Smith did or said with respect to flying saucers was based on the information from Sarbacher that UFOs were from outer space. Smith was not out to prove that they were extraterrestrial, because he already "knew." His goal was to solve the propulsion problem.

Solandt took the opposite position to Smith at this first meeting and spoke about a terrestrial-based theory for UFO reports. He said that an aeronautical engineer, John Frost of A.V. Roe Canada Limited, believed the objects were of Russian origin. Frost had perhaps based this conclusion on his knowledge of alleged German flying saucer designs from the war. Solandt felt that Frost's ideas were to be seriously considered because even if the saucers were extraterrestrial, Solandt believed they would still have to follow conventional aerodynamic theory in the earth's atmosphere. Besides, he thought that a new type of high-speed design might evolve from Frost's work.

When the first meeting of Project Second Storey came to a close, it was decided that Dr. Millman from the Dominion Observatory would be the chairman at future meetings. The group agreed to strive to produce a UFO-reporting questionnaire, develop interrogation procedures, and establish a standard approach for recording and analyzing reports. The DRB would remain in an advisory capacity and the collection of reports would be through field organizations such as the military and the RCMP. The group was essentially formalizing what had begun in 1950, and the new questionnaire would in fact become a refinement of the one developed in 1950.

At the second meeting, held on April 24, 1952, the group decided that the U.S. authorities should be formally approached for a possible exchange of information on the subject of UFOs. This was to be done through the DRB member in Washington.

A review of the minutes from succeeding meetings shows only that some inquiries were made and a summary of Project Blue Book was received from the USAF. There was no mention of Sarbacher, the committee under Bush, or anything else related to retrieved disks. It is also not known if Bremner was the contact man in question.

At the group's subsequent meeting, in May 1952, the official title of Project Second Storey was adopted. The important part of this meeting was the instruction Solandt gave to Millman: "The committee and all deliberations are classified as <u>Confidential</u> and must be so treated. Contacts with the press or public are <u>not</u> to be made."[4] Interestingly, Wilbert Smith's name is also underlined in the minutes of this meeting.

Solandt gave no reason for his position but it probably harkened back to his earlier request to Smith that the U.S. classification on these matters be respected. What is peculiar about the directive not to speak to the media is that there was every indication Project Second Storey was to be open to the public, from whom it would solicit reports of sightings. Here again one wonders if perhaps two conclusions would be drawn. One conclusion would be for public consumption and the other for the government.

The committee, with considerable input from Smith, finally developed a suitable questionnaire with accompanying instructions. This was to replace the questionnaire developed and used in 1950. Smith even conducted an experiment for the group, to help determine the validity of reported sightings, i.e., how reliable witnesses would be in reporting what they saw.

Under the auspices of his Department, Smith launched a twelve-foot diameter meteorological balloon from the site of the agricultural experimental farm in Ottawa. Attached to the balloon was a thirty-second magnesium flare. The launch time was

9:52 p.m., on the evening of September 8, 1952. The press was not notified. Smith was hoping that as witnesses called in their sightings, he could determine how accurately the balloon's features were being reported.

The actual result was that no witnesses came forward with reports and Smith was unable to perform the validation he had hoped for. Any one of a number of things could have gone wrong but it may have been simply that, perhaps in the absence of noise as an attention getter, no one happened to be looking up at the time. Alternatively, maybe the object was recognized for what it was, a balloon, and promptly dismissed as nothing unusual worth reporting. In fact, Smith could perhaps have made use of the sightings of the Chant meteor. Although no one knew exactly what it was, there were enough sightings across Canada and the United States which could have been used for comparative purposes.

Smith soon became dissatisfied with the Project Second Storey committee. Whereas he wanted investigations and analysis, the committee was interested only in receiving and cataloging sightings. He had made several recommendations, few of which were accepted because they involved expanding the scope of the committee beyond the range in which its members were interested. He believed that apart from Millman, none of the other members, who were mostly intelligence types, had any scientific interest in the saucers. Though Smith continued attending the meetings, he pressed ahead independently with Project Magnet, his own study and analysis of the reports of UFOs, in hopes of finding clues to their methods of propulsion.

Although the actual minutes of it appear not to exist, a final meeting of Project Second Storey was held on February 25, 1954. At this meeting it was concluded that the sightings did not "lend themselves to a scientific method of investigation."[5] Despite his efforts and the conclusions reached in his report, Smith had apparently been unable to convince the Project Second Storey members of the value of the work. The project secretary informed the DAI of the group's conclusions. Oatway also noted, however, that while reports would not be analyzed, they would continue to be collected, and Millman wrote a summary memorandum expressing this conclusion.

According to Arthur Bray, a draft of the minutes of this last meeting was made available to him. In it there was no discussion of Smith's final Project Magnet report, but as it turned out, Smith's conclusions were not supported by the Project Second Storey committee or by his own Department of Transport.

For his part, Solandt remained silent on Smith's conclusions, noting only that from information he had obtained in the United States, it was unnecessary to put any more manpower into the study of UFOs. In fact, what happened was that Smith had just been discredited (see Chapter Three) when Project Second Storey failed to endorse his conclusions.

Enter Peter Millman. Millman did not subscribe to a belief in the extraterrestrial hypothesis and may have been chosen as chairman of Project Second Storey because of his skepticism. Or he may have been selected because it was known that he had already formulated a conclusion. In fact, Millman was the Canadian equivalent of the late Dr. Allen Hynek, professor of astronomy at Northwestern University and early hard-nosed skeptic of UFOs. Hynek had been asked to be a consultant to Project Sign in 1948 and remained as consultant to the USAF and Project Blue Book for about twenty more years, completely debunking UFO reports, before he slowly began to change his mind. He would later write that the air force attitude was to debunk and that he believed some of the best-reported cases bypassed him and Blue Book and went directly to some higher authority.

Putting Millman in charge of Second Storey was an excellent way for Solandt to distance himself from Smith and the entire subject, if that was his intention. Smith had recognized that Project Second Storey was essentially a do-nothing committee. Even Brant, Smith's boss, criticized Second Storey and came down on the Defence Research Board for leaving all the investigating to Smith and the Department of Transport.

If there was any kind of cover-up in the Smith affair, it might have been by the DRB and the liaison staff in Washington. Just what did Solandt find out when he made his inquiries in Washington? What did Arnold Wright or Gordon E. Cox know? Why had the Minister of National Defence requested a joint committee be established to study the matter? What did the people in the Joint Intelligence Committee know? The questions go on, but are not answered in the files thus far uncovered.

Wilbert Smith developed brain cancer in 1961 and died the following year. It is possible that proof of the existence of UFOs as interplanetary vehicles died with him, and his legacy consists largely of unanswered questions.

Dr. Solandt passed away in the early nineties. He remained adamant that he had no knowledge of crashed disks or alien bodies.

At that first meeting of Project Second Storey back in April 1952, Solandt had countered Smith's extraterrestrial hypothesis and spoke of the work of John Frost of A.V. Roe. Frost was hoping to build a flying saucer using conventional technology based on information obtained from Nazi Germany.

On June 7, 1952, the following article appeared in a German newspaper, the *Duesseldorfer Nachrichten*, entitled "Flying Saucers German V 7?" It quoted *France Soir*, a Paris newspaper, as stating that flying saucers were the result of German designs towards the end of the war.

. . . a German V Waffen Engineer, Dr. Richard Miethe . . . said: "I dare to state that flying saucers, which appear in the sky, were constructed in Germany according to my own specifications . . ." The German Engineer is supposed to have said that a new design of the V arms in the shape of disks capable of travelling 21,000 kilometres [13,000 miles] and equipped with radar and called V7 was ready for mass production at the end of the war. These guided disks were successfully used over the Baltic Sea.[6]

If this article was true, could these disks have been the "Foo fighters" of the Second World War? Were Spatz and Goy legitimate? And just as important, what has become of the design now?

Five

Project Y:
The Avrocar

"A small fraction of <u>black world</u> engineers and scientists, [so called because they work on top-secret projects] are encouraged by recent government commitments to open intelligence agency files . . . In voicing their views, this small group of scientific professionals dared to break a code of silence that rivals the Mafia's, and several individuals claim they have suffered accordingly. . . . 'Once you are in they don't let you go,' an engineer said."[1]

Aviation Week & Space Technology, March 9, 1992

John C. M. Frost, mentioned earlier as one who took seriously the existence of German saucer designs, was a British aeronautical engineer who had been involved in the development of the CF-100, an all-weather Canadian military fighter. He was made chief design engineer for special projects at A. V. Roe Canada Limited (later Avro) in 1952. Those who knew him describe him as a somewhat unorthodox individual, with an intense interest in the subject of flying saucers. It is said that he carried a scrap book of flying saucer sightings, and he likely knew Wilbert Smith because their mutual supporter was Dr. Omond Solandt of the Canadian Defence Research Board.

In April 1952 Frost co-authored a paper with T. D. Earl entitled "Proposal for a Gas Turbine Propelled Aircraft of Circular Plan Form." He followed this in July of that year with "Project Y: An All-Wing Supersonic Aeroplane."[2] His goal was to design, build, and fly a flying saucer. Oddly, in spite of the fact that the Canadian government expressed minimal interest in his project, Frost noted that Solandt was instrumental in interesting the United States Air Force, through General D. C. Putt, then head of the USAF Air Research and Development Command.

In addition to finding out if it could in fact be done, the USAF, or perhaps Dr. Vannevar Bush's secret group, may have had other reasons for seeing the saucer built. Writing in Ideal's *UFO* magazine in 1978, Lieutenant Colonel (USAF) George Edwards (retired) claimed that the saucer was being developed as a cover, not as a supersonic, man-made saucer:

> Although we were not cut in on it, we know that the AF was secretly test-flying a real alien spacecraft. The VZ-9 [Frost's saucer] was to be a "cover," so the Pentagon would have an explanation whenever people reported seeing a saucer in flight.[3]

Major Donald Keyhoe expounded this theme in his 1960 book, *Flying Saucers: Top Secret.* He cited an incident that occurred on August 1, 1955. A witness in Ohio reported a large, circular object with a red light on the rim. At one point the object stopped in mid-air and shone two beams of light to the ground. It made no noise as it then proceeded to pass over the witness's house and speed away.

In 1956 a friend of the witness who was told of the encounter made a report to the Air Technical Intelligence Center (ATIC). Shortly thereafter, a military man with the rank of major visited the witness and his family. The major showed them what appeared to be a picture of a flying saucer and said it was built at A. V. Roe in Canada. It was the Avro craft they had seen, he assured them. He even tried to persuade them to sign a statement to that effect. They did not sign and instead reported the incident to the National Investigations Committee on Aerial Phenomena (NICAP), a civilian organization of which Keyhoe was to become director. In a subsequent book Keyhoe noted that the Avro saucer as cover story was again brought up by the air force in 1965 just before a House Armed Services Committee hearing into the whole subject of UFOs and the air force's handling of reported sightings.

Whether it was a ruse for hiding the true secret behind the saucers or not, news of Project Y was eventually leaked to the press. The *Toronto Star* carried a feature article on February 11, 1953, under the headline "Takes Off Straight Up Report Malton 'Flying Saucer' to Do 1,500 MPH":

Highly secret reports of a Canadian "flying saucer" are circulating among British and U.S. defence scientists . . . the craft is designed to take off vertically, fly horizontally at about 1,500 miles an hour, and make use of the gyroscopic effect of a revolving power plant to acquire stability . . . Western scientists must consider the possibility that Soviet Russia has carried similar developments to a more advanced stage . . . Crawford Gordon, president of A.V. Roe, said, "No comment" . . .[4]

The reference to gyroscopic stability is most interesting, as it parallels the earlier comments by Goy. Moreover, the sentence referring to Russian developments is the reason Goy had written his letter in the first place, a year before. Other newspapers carried artist's drawings of the proposed Avro disk, and the U.S. press dubbed it the "Avro Omega." Avro was at this time also embarking on the development of the futuristic Avro Arrow interceptor.

Frost's Project Y report described a somewhat semicircular or horseshoe-shaped vehicle supposedly capable of flying at 1,400 mph and reaching altitudes of over 60,000 feet. In describing a highly secret project, the newspapers had amazingly gotten it just about right.

With money from Solandt and the Defence Research Board, as well as from Avro itself, work on the design continued. With its landing gear extended, Project Y sat at an angle on its tail. It was apparently nicknamed the "Praying Mantis" or the "Flying Manta." Frost reasoned that taking off and landing in this position would be difficult, if not out-and-out dangerous. The concept was abandoned.

Frost next decided to explore a straight vertical takeoff and landing idea, doing away with the landing gear and using the underside of the vehicle itself as a landing pad. This resulted in the completely circular flying saucer design and the accident of unrealized discovery. Given the conventional method of propulsion being considered, Avro had in fact unknowingly discovered the principle of the ground cushion effect. Had Avro then put a skirt around the saucer, they would have had a hovercraft years before anyone else. Frost would later admit:

It is unfortunate that our sights were set on developing a supersonic vertical takeoff aircraft when Avro stumbled on the ground cushion, otherwise we might have paid more attention to its possible uses as an amphibious surface vehicle . . . we missed its potential as a method of improving the performance of water-borne craft . . .[5]

In June 1954 Avro produced a report entitled "Project Y2: Flat Vertical Take-Off Supersonic Gyroplane."[6] The report described a circular craft using conventional engines for power, with a cockpit in the center of the craft. Intakes for forward flight were located at the top and bottom of the craft, forward of the cockpit. For vertical takeoff, intakes were located in an inner ring on the upper surface. Exhausts were located on the perimeter of the craft.

During takeoff, air would flow through slots in the upper surface of the disk to radially mounted engines which would eject their exhaust to the periphery of the craft. At this point the exhaust would be deflected downwards by a series of vanes or flaps. This method of redirecting the exhaust by strategically placing a flap in the airstream was known as the "Coanda effect," named after its discoverer, Henri Coanda, a Romanian engineer who had been linked to the German saucer experiments during the war. The effect helped to create the ground cushion. On landing, this ground cushion would act to dampen any sudden impact. In forward flight, the same flaps would redirect the exhaust backwards with air provided from the forward-facing intakes. The craft was expected to attain speeds of between 1,720 and 2,300 mph and reach a maximum height of between 71,000 and 80,600 feet, with a capability to hover as high as 18,000 feet.

Avro funded the development, assisted by $300,000 from the DRB until 1954. This was soon to change, however. In late August, 1954, General O. P. Weyland, Commander USAF at

Tactical Air Command, Langley AFB, visited Avro and was given a thorough briefing on Project Y2. Before he left he expressed his desire to join the venture.

Further discussions were held with General Putt through the DRB. The result was the award of a $758,000 contract from the USAF in early 1955. The contract was to extend through to August 1956 and the project title was changed to Project 1794. The contract allowed for supersonic testing at the wind tunnel of the Massachusetts Institute of Technology, subsonic and hover tests at the wind tunnel at the Wright Air Development Center, and various other tests back at Avro. As the test results proved favorable, Avro established another project, Project P.V. (Private Venture) 704 in January 1956. This project allowed for development of the propulsion and control system test rigs. P.V. 704 was to extend into 1958 at an estimated cost of $5,000,000.

While work was progressing, United States Secretary of the Air Force Donald Quarles noted in a public statement on October 25, 1955, that the USAF was engaged in the design of a circular craft with Avro Canada Ltd. Quarles indicated that such craft might "give the illusion of the so-called flying saucer"[7] and that the government would endeavor to keep the public informed of such developments, within the bounds of security. Quarles seems to have been preparing to explain away any flying saucer sightings as being those of the Avro craft.

In March 1957 the USAF continued its interest by extending Project 1794 through into October 1958. The project name was now changed to Research System 606A (Weapon System 606A in some papers) and the contract was to be worth $1,600,000. In fact, the Canadian government had supplied $300,000 between 1952 and 1953, Avro had provided $2,500,000 up to March 1958, and the USAF had contributed $785,000 in 1954 and now $1,815,000 in 1957. The new contract included further studies in the subsonic wind tunnel, development of the combustion system for supersonic flight, and studies involving operational considerations. Approximately 1,000 hours of tests had been completed in the wind tunnels and ground cushion tests using upwards of seventy-five models had all been completed at Avro. As well, testing had begun on the propulsion system.

Also in 1957, members of the U.S. Army visited Avro on September 26 and 27. The army required a craft with greater mobility and was interested in vehicles that could fly close to the surface of the ground — as Project Y could in ground cushion mode. They explained that development contracts totaling $1,700,000 had been given to various companies, including Chrysler, Aerophysics, Goodyear, Piasecki, and Hiller, but that the army was not happy with any of the designs. They were hoping Avro could provide the required vehicle.

Avro personnel were then invited to brief General Gavin at a meeting at the Pentagon on November 29, 1957. What Avro proposed was a subsonic vehicle based on the Project Y design. The craft was featured in a report entitled "U.S. Army Requirement for a New Family of Air Vehicles," dated November 26, 1957.

By April 1958 the USAF, the U.S. Army, and U.S. Office of the Secretary of Defense had agreed to establish an integrated USAF/U.S. Army program with joint funding but under the management of the air force. The program would satisfy the army's subsonic requirement and be a first step towards realizing the supersonic USAF flying saucer. It was agreed that Project 606A would be reoriented to study the simpler, subsonic army vehicle and that Avro would therefore stop work on the supersonic P.V. 704 in favor of first completing this one. The U.S. Army would arrange funding to procure two vehicles for completion of the full test program. The value of the joint USAF/U.S. Army contracts for fabrication and testing of the prototype vehicles was set at $4,432,497. And so the Avromobile — more popularly known as the Avrocar — was born.

Under a new USAF contract, AF 33(600)-3796, the first prototype aircraft, designated U.S. Army VZ-9 AV, was built and rolled out in May 1959. Under Supplemental Agreement No. 1 of the contract, the second vehicle was authorized and rolled out in August 1959. Between June 9 and October 7, 1959, the first vehicle underwent a thirty-two-hour static rig test at Avro in Malton, Ontario. The prototype was then sent to the NASA Ames wind tunnel for full-scale wind tunnel tests commencing in April 1960. A second round of wind tunnel testing commenced in April 1961. The first free-flight test, conducted on the second vehicle, occurred on November 12, 1959, with additional tests made in January 1960.

The Avrocar was 18 feet in diameter, with a weight of 2,820 pounds empty and a takeoff gross weight of 5,680 pounds, including 840 pounds of fuel and a 190-pound pilot. It was further described technically as follows:

> The Avrocar was equipped with a 5ft diameter fan situated in its center, exhausting via an internal duct system to a peripheral nozzle. The fan was driven by means of a tip turbine which used the exhaust from three [Continental] J69-T-9 engines . . . The three exhausts from the J69 engines each occupied 120 degrees of the turbine inlet area . . . The hot exhaust from the turbine was mixed with the cold flow from the fan in a duct immediately below the fan. This duct passes from the bottom of the fan beneath the cockpits, engine bays, and cargo compartments to the peripheral nozzle around the circumference of the vehicle . . .[8]

A speed of over 300 mph was predicted. All seemed well until the first actual tests were carried out on the specially designed test rig. It became apparent then that the central fan was not allowing as much air to flow through as had been originally calculated. The fix would require structural modifications, so the decision was made to continue with the tests and perform the changes later. This meant that with reduced thrust, the Avrocar could not hover using the ground cushion effect, and instead would rise only a few feet off the ground. A second problem ensued, this time with the intakes for the three engines. The intake design was causing the engines to overheat, necessitating further design changes and losses in thrust of up to 5 percent.

Then came the various instabilities:

> . . . a stable or near stable ground cushion in pitch and roll was essential . . . The design . . . therefore, included an outer peripheral jet, with the addition of a central jet . . . [There was] considerable dynamic instability [but] . . . the situation was eventually cured by increasing the strength of the central jet, and also increasing the sensitivity of the aircraft stabilizing system . . . The Avrocar is circular in plan, the engines are evenly disposed, as is the fuel and, to some extent, the two operators; the center of gravity is therefore close to the center of the plan area. The aerodynamic center for a circular planform was found to be 28% of the root chord. The wing will, therefore, have negative static margin, which follows that it is statically and dynamically unstable in aerodynamic flight and must be stabilized by artificial means . . .[9]

The solution to this problem of inherent instability was to develop an artificial means of stabilization. The more advanced, electronic form of artificial stabilization had been successfully implemented on the advanced Avro Arrow interceptor which Avro was also developing. Unfortunately, Frost did not yet trust the electronic stabilization which in later years was to be successfully employed in aircraft such as the SR-71, F/A-18 Hornet, and Stealth. He chose instead to develop a mechanical means of stabilization.

In August 1960 the Avrocar was displayed for the press. It traveled at 35 mph but observers could see that the instabilities still existed, even though it successfully traversed various types of terrain. An appraisal of the Avrocar by the Air Force Flight Test Center at Edwards Air Force Base concluded the following:

> Performance, stability and control of the Avrocar in its present configuration prevents accelerating in ground effect to a free air flight speed. Full scale wind tunnel results indicate that sufficient control is available to conduct a transition into high speed flight (about 100 knots IAS maximum), provided that 35 to 40 knots can be obtained with the focussing ring control system . . .[10]

The report went on to list the areas that would require modification in order for the Avrocar to achieve this transition to high-speed flight.

Several modifications were completed by April 1961 and the results were satisfactory. Engineer Arnold Rose, who worked on the design, explained to this author in 1991 that the problems had finally been worked out. Frost himself stated in 1961 that the results showed that aerodynamic flight would soon be possible and that full-scale flight tests were set for the next phase of the project. All that was needed was additional funding from the USAF/U.S. Army. The money never came. Perhaps the publicity surrounding the Avrocar had already achieved what some say was the primary aim: the creation of a smoke screen for flying saucer sightings. Or perhaps the design was taken to the United States for further development. It would not be the first time that this had been done. In any event, since there was no money coming from the Canadian government either, the project was abandoned by Avro.

Avro Aircraft was responsible for the technically successful Jetliner in 1949, the first commercial jet transport to fly in North America. This was followed by the subsonic CF-100 and, finally, by the supersonic, technically advanced Avro Arrow interceptor in 1959. The Jetliner project, with offers pending from several U.S. airline companies, including interest from Howard Hughes and TWA, was inexplicably canceled in 1953. The Arrow, after successfully completing several flight trials and on the verge of establishing world speed and altitude records, was canceled in 1959, with the five flying prototypes and others in various stages of assembly being blowtorched out of existence.

Now, with no further contracts forthcoming on the saucer, Avro itself closed its doors for good. Avro's employees found their way to the United States and made their marks at places such as Boeing, Lockheed, and especially NASA. The documentation from the Arrow program also made its way south. As for the two prototype Avrocars, one found its way to Fort Eustis in Virginia while the other wound up in a Smithsonian storage area. One of Canada's largest and most progressive corporations was no more.

Questions have always remained as to whether the technological effort on the Avrocar was indeed discontinued or was picked up in the United States under a "black program." The term "black program" is used to describe secret development programs whose existence is kept from the general public and even from other government agencies. Examples of such programs include the U-2 spy plane of the 1950s, its successor, the SR-71 Blackbird, and most recently the Stealth aircraft such as the F-117A and the B-2 bomber. Undoubtedly, the atomic-powered aircraft mentioned by Bremner was being developed as a black program as well. Personnel working on such programs are not only sworn to secrecy but may also have their human rights threatened in an attempt to silence them. Did the Avrocar evolve?

In the early nineties speculation was rampant that a new "black," hypersonic aircraft was being test-flown by the United States Air Force. This speculation was based on reported sightings of incredibly fast-moving, triangular-shaped aircraft with unusual engine noises and strange contrails of smoke resembling knots along a string or "doughnuts on a rope." The speculation was further fueled by a 1985 Pentagon budget document requesting funds for a number of programs, including one called "Aurora." It has been presumed that Aurora is, or was, the code name for this hypersonic aircraft, the successor to the SR-71 Blackbird.

Interestingly, evidence for the existence of this new aircraft also came from a U.S. geological survey, which picked up unidentified sonic booms across southern California. Naturally, the USAF and all concerned have denied the existence of such aircraft. As explained in *Jane's Defense Weekly*, however, "The USAF's credibility is undermined by the fact that the DOD authorizes disseminating misleading information."[11] In other words, to keep information secret, the USAF is authorized to orchestrate a disinformation campaign. An example of the effectiveness of such a campaign occurred during the development of the U-2. For years, while the U-2 aircraft was overflying and spying on other countries, most governments and the public believed the cover story that this plane was simply involved in weather mapping and related meteorological work.

One of the ways such programs are disguised, for the purpose of obtaining government funding, is through the use of multiple-project code names which are not easily tracked. Or, such projects are sometimes hidden as part of the development of other projects. For example, it was noted in *Jane's* that the National Aero-space Plane (NASP), a project to develop a commercial hypersonic passenger aircraft, may have been used as a cover for the development of Aurora.

According to *Jane's*, NASP was an unclassified program focusing research on Mach 8 performance, a difficult goal to achieve. Therefore, initial work on a propulsion system was aimed at achieving speeds somewhat lower than Mach 8 but much faster than anything else. This was not unlike the decision to develop a subsonic Avrocar first, before moving on to the supersonic Project Y.

Jane's points out that the lower-speed aspects of the propulsion system development for NASP were in fact classified and not open to public scrutiny like the rest of the project. In other words, the lower-speed development might in fact have been for the Aurora but under the auspices of the NASP project. With a lower-speed Aurora completed, NASP would be allowed to "fizzle" out as currently unattainable. Meanwhile, Aurora would be flying, unknown to all but a privileged few. Granted, its speed might not be Mach 8, but Mach 4 or above would best anything else flying.

Such state-of-the-art aircraft would require advanced methods of propulsion. The "combined cycle" engine, which combines the elements of a ramjet engine with those of a rocket and turbine engine, was what was speculated for Aurora. It is said that such an engine can power an aircraft at any speed up to Mach 6. Combined cycle engines were invented in the late 1950s and further experimented with in the 1960s by Dr. Fred Billig of the applied physics laboratory of Johns Hopkins University. Billig noted that these engines were most efficient, being able to recover and utilize energy that conventional engines would lose. It is conceivable that while John Frost was using conventional engines and was ironing out the stability problems with the Avrocar, the USAF was fully intending to carry on the development of Project Y using the combined cycle engine or some other experimental means of propulsion.

The declassification on March 29, 1995, of technical report TR-AC-47 from the Air Technical Intelligence Center at Wright-Patterson Air Force Base, Ohio, illustrates that Project Y was part of a black program development. The report is titled "Joint ATIC-WADC Report on Project Silver Bug," listed as Project No. 9961, and dated February 15, 1955. Before the release of this document, the project code name "Silver Bug" had not appeared in any other correspondence or literature dealing with Project Y or the Avrocar. The Avro flying saucer development program, then, has carried the following names: U.S. Army VZ-9 AV or Avrocar for public consumption; Weapon System 606A or Project 1794 for dealings with Canada on the supersonic model; Project Y, Project Y2, and P.V. 704 for aspects of the project internal to Avro; and finally, Silver Bug or Project 9961 for the supersonic version internal to the United States Air Force.

The Silver Bug report is essentially a copy of Frost's Y2 report with some interesting added discussion. It indicates that the project was not connected in any way with flying saucer stories even though the craft had a circular shape. The circular design resulted from engineering investigations to solve a specific problem. The report says a circular design would solve the requirement for "achieving dispersed base operations."[12] That is, with the craft's vertical takeoff and landing capability the need for special runways would be negligible, so that launch areas could be established anywhere, including the decks of submarines.

The report continues with the following:

> The ultimate purpose . . . is to correct the distorted picture presented in previous releases, both classified and unclassified, and to acquaint the intelligence community with the current state-of-the-art facts thereby alerting them to any air intelligence information which may become available indicating Soviet interest in this specialized field . . . There appears to be no fundamental reason why this proposal should not ultimately result in a weapon system . . . The technical information on this project should be followed by direct liaison between WADC and ATIC personnel . . . A collection effort should be initiated to determine whether the Soviet Bloc is or has been conducting research efforts on a similar project, when this work began, and the present state of the Soviet development.[13]

It appears that the United States was interested in seeing the advancement of Silver Bug but was also intent on finding out if the Soviets were in possession of similar or more advanced technology. Sightings like the one from Russia described below, as well as reports from people like Goy, may have been driving the Americans' interest in Soviet technology.

On October 5, 1955, three American officials, Senator Richard Russell (Republican, Georgia), Lieutenant Colonel E. U. Hathaway, the U.S. Army staff officer assigned to the Senate Armed Forces Committee, and Reuben Efron, consultant to the committee, witnessed two circular objects while traveling through Russia. The disks took off almost vertically and seemed to be emitting sparks. Their outer surface appeared to rotate slowly and they had two stationary lights on top. The U.S. officials believed they were witnessing secret Soviet aircraft based on the German wartime designs.

By the time the Avrocar project was terminated, the USAF may have either developed Silver Bug into a flying model or believed that enough information was now available to carry out a separate development. Alternatively, the difficulties encountered during the Avrocar experience may have persuaded them that the saucer design was unworkable. In either case, the publicity surrounding the Avrocar development appeared to deflect attention away from other U.S. developments and alien disks, at least for a short period.

In 1967 it was allegedly discovered that Project Silver Bug did achieve an advanced stage of development. Jack Pickett, a publisher of the *NCO Club* and *Officer Club* magazines, claims he saw four disk-shaped aircraft at Mac Dill Air Force Base: "Seen head-on they all appeared as the classic, so called flying saucer shape with the pilot/crew compartment appearing as a bubble, dead center."[14] Pickett said the craft were of varying sizes, ranging from 20 feet to anywhere from 50 to 75 feet across. They had air intake slots on either side of the crew compartment and exhausts underneath. He was told by the officer in charge that they had a very high airspeed, in excess of Mach 1, and that their altitude capability was extremely high, although no figures were mentioned. He was shown photographs of different formations in flight. The four craft he was allowed to view were awaiting a decision to be destroyed or sent to a museum. He was told that due to some maneuverability problems and the achievement of more practical designs, their development had been discontinued. These aircraft have been collectively dubbed "Lady Bug," but no further information on them has yet come to light.

It is an intriguing prospect that a flying saucer may have been built and is perhaps flying today. Still, that would not explain the thousands of sightings reported to Wilbert Smith and others over the years, nor does it answer Dr. Robert Sarbacher's assertions about crashed disks and alien beings. An examination of some of these reports, and of the continued efforts of Canada's Department of National Defence at collecting them even while telling the general public that the Department had no interest in the subject, is worth examining further.

Six

Project Magnet and the Fifties

"Interplanetary activity may well give us planetary peace. Once we discover Martian space ships hovering over earth's airspace, we will all come together."[1]

Lester B. Pearson, on accepting the Nobel Peace Prize in 1957

The 1950s were characterized by a cold war paranoia that manifested itself in an arms race, assorted spy scandals, the fear of all-out nuclear destruction, and in the United States, the House Un-American Activities Committee. People built backyard bomb shelters and learned survival techniques. The Rosenbergs became the first U.S. civilians to be executed for espionage.

The 1950s also saw the increasing popularity of the science fiction genre in books, film, and of course, television, which was rapidly becoming America's number-one entertainment medium. Ray Bradbury's *The Martian Chronicles* ushered in the decade, while the very popular television program *The Twilight Zone* ushered it out.

Whether or not connected to the red scare, to experimental military hardware such as the Avrocar and Project Y, or to the growth of science fiction, UFO sightings were common in the 1950s. Projects Magnet and Second Storey ran their course, and the public continued to make reports. But not all the sightings could be explained away. The following are typical of the reports contained in the Project Magnet file during those years.

On May 1, 1952, in Ottawa, a round, bright light streaked across the southern horizon at approximately 9:30 p.m. The light was visible for twelve seconds before vanishing. It was witnessed by six people in Ottawa and Aylmer. Calculations placed the object at 12,000 feet, traveling at a speed of 3,600 miles per hour, with a diameter of some 400 feet. Its color was white. No sound was heard. Just prior to this sighting, two other people had witnessed an orange object in the shape of an ellipse. It appeared to hover for some time before vanishing. Mars was in the sky at the time but at a different location than the reported object and therefore could not account for the sighting. At 9:15 p.m. a bright light was seen moving east to west across the southern sky. Reported by an observer in Smiths Falls, the description given was similar to that provided by the Ottawa observers.

It should be mentioned that sightings of both Mars and Venus are often given as explanations for UFOs. Both of these planets are quite bright and Mars often twinkles a reddish color. Atmospheric conditions, including rapidly blowing clouds, can give the illusion that the planets are moving. But these sightings could not have been either of the two planets.

On June 15, 1952, in the sky southeast of Halifax, Nova Scotia, a large, silver, disk-shaped object was seen by a meteorological assistant. The object traveled southwest for some thirty seconds and was at an altitude of 5,000 to 8,000 feet. It ascended vertically and disappeared into the clouds. Its speed was estimated at 800 miles per hour, faster than a conventional aircraft also in the air at the time.

On July 25, 1952, seven objects in a "V" formation were seen traveling south over Ottawa. It was 8:00 a.m. and the objects were bright blue, self-luminous, and round in shape. At 11:45 a.m. two additional objects were seen moving southeast. This incident occurred in the midst of the famous UFO sightings over Washington, D.C. (one of which is described below).

On July 19, 1952, and again on July 26, UFOs were picked up on air traffic control radar over Washington. Visual sightings were also made by commercial pilots in the air at the time. Interceptors were scrambled and at least one of the pilots made visual contact. He reportedly described the objects as blue-white lights. At one point he said they encircled his aircraft. Publicly, the explanation given was that temperature inversions had caused the radar blips. As noted by Timothy Good in *Above Top Secret*, however, a number of individuals in the intelligence community believed that the "objects sighted may possibly be from another planet."[2]

Wilbert Smith was sent a piece of metal allegedly retrieved from one of the disks, for analysis.

On August 27, 1952, an unidentified object was seen over the RCAF station in Macdonald, Manitoba, by two RCAF meteorological observers. It was 4:45 a.m. The object was disk-shaped, with shadows across it as though it had an irregular surface. It was shiny and aluminum or silver in color and appeared to be directly over the airport. It made two turns and then shot off towards the northwest within a second. No sound was heard. The object had apparently been caught in the rotating beacon of the tower before it shot away. Both observers felt it could not have been a bird or conventional aircraft.

On December 31, 1952, at 3:00 a.m., a sighting came in from Regina, Saskatchewan, of a luminous, circular object traveling down towards the horizon. The object was spotted by the meteorological officer and the air traffic controller at the Regina airport. Twenty minutes later a similar object was sighted by the same observers. This one seemed to fluctuate, appearing larger as it got brighter. Both objects were unrelated to an aircraft that was also in the vicinity.

The Regina area was rife with such reports, prompting a letter from the controller at the Department of Transport to the Aviation Forecast Office in Regina, dated January 21, 1953. The letter noted that reports submitted by the Forecast Office had been substantiated by other witnesses: "These reports would appear to indicate that some unknown objects are landing and taking off and that the activities seem to be concentrated in the Regina-Moose Jaw general area."[3]

The letter went on to state that all weather observers in Regina give special attention to the reporting of any sightings and that airport control officers and others working outdoors do likewise. The matter was to be treated as confidential, with no newspaper involvement. All pilots operating through Regina, as well as the weather observers working for Canadian Pacific Airlines, were to be apprised of the situation.

On March 18, 1954, after the last meeting of Second Storey, a report came in from Manitoba. At 10:25 p.m., a silver, match-like object was seen by two conservation officers from the Department of Mines and Resources. The object was in view for twenty minutes or more and was described as about 100 feet in length and eight feet in diameter (thickness?). It would move slowly to the east for about two miles, stop, and move back to the west. The object would also change from being horizontal to vertical and back to horizontal, before moving east or west.

UFO phenomena were also occupying government minds outside of North America. A letter dated November 29, 1954, and addressed to Group Captain Edwards, Director of Air Intelligence, illustrates that Canadians and Americans were not the only ones sighting UFOs. The letter was sent by Colonel Mario Bucchi, Air Military and Naval Attache at the Italian Embassy in Ottawa. Colonel Bucchi indicated that Italian authorities had previously discounted reports of flying saucers as fantasy or optical phenomena. Now, however, sightings had become so frequent in Italy that the matter was being taken seriously. The first step in getting a handle on the subject was to determine the views of friendly countries like Canada.

A handwritten note on the letter asks the DAI if any information could be provided to Colonel Bucchi, but that it be "no higher than 'Confidential' on this subject . . ."[4] This is an odd notation, given the fact that according to the American Project Grudge report, there was supposed to be nothing to the sightings. One has to ask, why was there a restriction to another military government agency?

The reply to Colonel Bucchi ended up stating that although reports were being collected in Canada, there was no attempt to analyze them.

Italians, Americans, and Canadians were not the only ones who were mystified. The Department of National Defence was being kept apprised of UFO stories and sighting reports from other countries. These were gathered by the American Central Intelligence Agency. One report received from the CIA had actually been extracted from the *Morgon-Tidningen*, a Stockholm daily paper. On July 13, 1953, the paper reported:

Danish defense authorities take a serious view of the problem of flying saucers. The military experts are of the opinion that although most of the observations of flying saucers have turned out to be astronomical phenomena, there remain the reports of trained observers which, among other things, would seem to indicate that the saucers are dispatched from Soviet bases in the Arctic Ocean.[5]

The story goes on to say that the Danish Air Force Command wrote a report concerning sightings that had occurred in the air as well as in the water. The Danish sightings had been compared to reports of sightings in Norway and Finland. Several reports from those countries were noted, such as the one of the sighting over the Karup Airfield on Jutland. The object resembled an airplane but flew faster than any known type.

In northern Norway, a mysterious object was seen and an aircraft was sent to investigate but was not able to reach the object before it left at terrific speed. The conclusion was that the sightings over the Nordic countries could have been of aircraft from a Soviet base on an island in the Arctic Ocean even if they were of no known design. Additional reports came in from Corsica, France's African colonies, western Europe, and Israel.

A most interesting sighting occurred over Hokkaido, Japan, in January 1953. Colonel (RCAF) D. M. Blakeslee, the commanding officer of 27th FE Wing, was flying his F-84 Sabre at 25,000 feet when he saw an object off in the distance. He flew towards it and climbed to 32,000 feet, when he again saw the object below him but still off in the distance. He tried approaching it again but just as he was closing in, it literally disappeared. He did not see it climb, dive, or speed away. It simply vanished.

Blakeslee reported that he had the object in view for at least two minutes. It displayed a green, red, and white light along the edge of a "large horizontal body." The three lights appeared to rotate in a counterclockwise direction. Another F-84 pilot in the air at the time reported seeing the object also but felt that the three lights were revolving in a vertical direction. The operator in the control tower at Chitose-Hokkaido saw a similar object but it was not picked up on any radar.

On August 23, 1956, RCAF pilots again reported sighting mysterious objects. Squadron Leader Robert J. Childerhorse and Flight Lieutenant Ralph Innis were attempting to set a speed record across Canada. At an altitude of 36,000 feet over Fort Macleod in southern Alberta, Childerhorse saw and photographed a glowing, white, oval ball near some thunder clouds.

As the sightings continued, so did efforts to collect them. On December 4, 1956, the Canadian–United States Joint Communications Electronics Committee (Can.-U.S. JCEC) gave their approval to a paper for the Standardized Canadian–United States Communications Instructions for Reporting Vital Intelligence Sightings (CIRVIS/MERINT). The CIRVIS/MERINT system established procedures for providing information on vital intelligence sightings to air-defense forces from ships or aircraft operating outside the coverage of early warning radar systems. While the program was already in force in the United States, active participation by Canada was now sought.

"Vital Intelligence Sightings" included hostile or unidentified aircraft, missiles, hostile or unidentified submarines, surface vessels, and, of course, unidentified flying objects. The CIRVIS/MERINT procedure was essentially what was prescribed in the U.S. Joint Army Navy Air Force Publication, JANAP 146. In fact, as a product of JANAP 146(D) of February 1959, the Can.-U.S. JCEC developed the CIRVIS/MERINT reporting procedure poster, which listed agencies to whom reports should be sent. These included any Canadian military establishment,

RCMP post, Department of Fisheries representative, Hudson's Bay Company, Northern Radio-Equipment store, or Canadian telegraph office.

The Condon Committee, a group of scientists and researchers who studied UFOs in the sixties, stated that the term "unidentified flying object" in the CIRVIS/MERINT procedure simply meant any object puzzling to the observer or witness. This was an obvious attempt to play down the significance of the term "UFO" in the JANAP 146 document as referring to extraterrestrial craft.

The poster, however, provided pictorials for each class of object sighted. For UFOs a small drawing of a flying saucer was shown. It is very clear from this poster that "UFO" in the JANAP or CIRVIS/MERINT procedures meant an extraterrestrial spaceship and not just something an observer could not identify. If UFOs were simply misidentifications or misinterpretations, why did the U.S. military go to such lengths to include a specific category in their procedures, and why did Canada agree?

Seven

"Vital Intelligence Sightings" in the Sixties

"It is policy to investigate in detail reports of UFO's which cannot be readily identified as man-made or natural phenomena."

RCAF correspondence, February 25, 1964

On October 15, 1962, some minor amendments were made to the CIRVIS/MERINT procedure of JANAP 146(D) and the reporting of vital intelligence sightings (including UFOs). This document contained reporting procedures for civil and commercial aircraft, government and military aircraft, merchant vessels, government and military vessels, fishing vessels, military installations receiving reports from civilian or military observers, and other government or civilian agencies in receipt of such information. Reports were to be filed if, in the opinion of the observer, urgent defensive or investigative action might be required. It was further stipulated that each report had to indicate whether the object sighted was deemed a threat to the security of the United States and Canada and their forces. This, of course, leaves open the possibility that once a report was deemed not to be a threat, the matter could be dropped or perhaps passed to another authority.

Interestingly, the directive requested that every effort be made to obtain photographs. It even went so far as to say that film would be processed and one copy of each print, along with a new roll of film, would be given back to the individual. However, U.S. accounts of sightings are filled with incidents in which film was never returned, returned damaged, or altered in some way.

The address given for the submission of such photographs was the U.S. Director of Naval Intelligence, Washington, D.C., or the Director of Naval Intelligence, Department of National Defence, Ottawa. Lieutenant Commander James Stewart Bremner, the man who put Wilbert Smith in touch with Dr. Sarbacher, was of course navy, and it was a naval officer, Rear Admiral Tate, who had advised Bremner of the atomic-powered aircraft. It is conceivable that while the Director of Air Intelligence was at the front line, so to speak, to receive and answer reports, the hard case reports were actually being handled by Naval Intelligence in both countries.

In 1963, in response to a series of questions from Canada's Parliament, the Chief of the Air Staff responded that Canada did co-operate with the United States for the investigation of UFO reports. The investigation, if warranted, was "conducted by Air Defence Command. In the normal course of events NORAD Headquarters would receive a copy of the report."[1] He further stated that no code name was applied to such reports, and certainly not Project Magnet.

The reply stated that Project Magnet was headed by Wilbert Smith. Since Smith was a Department of Transport employee, any related files belonged to Transport and not the Department of National Defence, and therefore the availability of those files could not be counted upon. No mention of Project Second Storey appeared in the response. Thus, DND could successfully evade the issue by passing it on to Transport. But why would they want to? Is this evidence of a cover-up or was the department keeping the matter quiet on behalf of the Americans?

Certainly, other correspondence on file suggests evasive answers were being provided either to get pesky inquirers off the department's back or simply to avoid publicity. For example, the following was noted in one file: "The proposed reply . . . is quite lengthy and informative (though not specific) in the hope that it may discourage further inquiries . . ."[2] But instead the tactics would backfire and invite publicity, implying there was a cover-up.

On February 25, 1964, the RCAF finally stated:

> The RCAF, through the Air Officer Commanding Air Defence Command, is charged with the military investigation of unidentified flying object (UFO) reports. It is policy to investigate in detail reports of UFO's which cannot be readily identified as man-made or natural phenomena.[3]

For all the negativism of earlier correspondence, the RCAF was finally admitting to officially investigating, not just collecting, UFO reports. The letter added that all reports to date had been identified as either man-made or natural phenomena known to scientists but perhaps not the general public.

It is clear from the comment about natural phenomena that only a few scientists were aware that some rather extraordinary sightings existed, sightings which simply could not be explained away. Even Dr. Allen Hynek, noted astronomer and special consultant to Project Blue Book, was stumped by some reports.

The reason for keeping the reports classified was, according to the memo, because they were treated as personal correspondence between the observers and the department. It may have also been because Part 2 of JANAP 146 made it an offense to disclose reports, by authority of the Canadian Official Secrets Act.

In a separate letter dated August 14, the Department of National Defence indicated that the procedures of JANAP 146(D) were being followed. Again, it was stated that most sightings could be explained by natural phenomena such as meteorites or optical effects, and that some reports were obviously figments of the imagination. Unlike the earlier correspondence, however, which suggested that all reports had been explained, this one said "most." No hint is given as to how many unexplained reports there might have been.

In 1965 the department was approached by the Canadian Broadcasting Corporation (CBC), which sought the department's participation in a segment on UFOs. The reply from the Director of Information Services to the DND Office of Information in Manitoba stated only that Headquarters did not wish to become involved with the CBC. It urged the Manitoba office to tactfully say no and to provide the CBC with a standard letter which was being used to answer queries about UFOs.

After 1965 it is unclear as to who in DND was handling UFO reports. Arthur Bray reports that the responsibility was transferred from Air Defence Command (ADC) to Canadian Forces Headquarters and that in the transition the files of ADC were destroyed. According to a paper on file, the Director of Air Intelligence took responsibility for coordinating any action or investigation of sightings. The paper notes that Professor J. C. Arnell, the scientific deputy chief of technical services, was the one who was handling reported sightings. In the spring of 1966 this responsibility was moved to the Director of Operations, perhaps in response to the procedures contained in the newly released JANAP 146(E).

For a phenomenon which government insisted did not exist, UFOs were certainly keeping both the Americans and Canadians busy. In October 1966 Canadian Forces Administrative Order (CFAO) 71-6, "Reporting of Unidentified Flying Objects," was made official. The order outlined the format in which reports were to be submitted to National Defence Headquarters. Specifically, the reports were to include as much information as possible with respect to the date and time of the sighting, weather conditions, identification of the principal witness and others, descriptions of the sighting, the duration of the sighting, and any other relevant information.

By November 1967 the Director General of Operations had decided that UFO information would be made available to personnel and organizations whose job it was to "inform the public and to further the scientific and objective research into UFOs." This change of policy was due to the widespread publicity being given to UFO phenomena at the time. The Director wanted to "avoid giving the impression that DND is 'hiding something' and attempting to suppress the release of UFO information . . ."[4]

In December 1967 the DND Director of Operations issued the following summary of procedures then in place. The Canadian Forces had the aforementioned CFAO directive, as well as a second one, CFAO 71-1, for the reporting of meteorites and fireballs. The RCMP had also adopted a similar procedure. It was further explained that in the past, Air Defence Command, in co-operation with the North American Air Defense Command (NORAD), was the office interested in unidentified flying objects, obviously from a security perspective.

ADC, like the American authorities, had found no reason to believe that UFOs posed a threat to the national security of Canada. They in no way interfered with Canada's defensive capability. Therefore the responsibility for handling these reports was handed over to headquarters in Ottawa. What this means is that the existence of UFOs and their point of origin was not of concern, but their modus operandi was, if it should pose a threat.

Headquarters divided the reports into two categories. Category one reports were of objects classified as meteorites and fireballs. Reports concerning these were sent to the National Research Council (NRC) Meteorite Centre for further analysis. Reports under category two were further divided into classes A, B, and C. Class A was reserved for reports warranting a formal investigation. Class B was for sightings that contained interesting information but warranted nothing further. Class C was reserved for reports considered to have little value.

Class A investigations might begin with an interview of the witness(es) and could eventually involve the RCMP, NRC, Defence Photographic Interpretation Centre, RCMP crime laboratories, and any other agencies that could assist. Of the 190 UFO reports collected between January 1 and November 30, 1967, only nine were designated class A. One of those class A reports concerned the famous case of Stefan Michalak, which occurred on May 20, 1967. The Michalak case will be dealt with in detail in Chapter Eight, based on the official DND and RCMP reports since declassified after an access request by this author.

A possibly related incident, and also one of the nine class A reports, occurred at 11:00 p.m. on the night of June 18, 1967, less than a month after the Michalak case. Mr. R. Greene was ferrying members of a family from Clear Water Bay, Shoal Lake, Ontario, to their home on the other side of the lake, when they saw a bright object hovering 50 feet above the tree tops and about a mile away. Unable to identify the object, Greene turned the boat in its direction for a closer look. When the object suddenly descended and came towards the boat, they headed for shore at full speed and got out of the boat. Noticing that the object had returned to its original position, they got back in the boat and made a second attempt at investigating it. When it again headed straight for them, they sped off to the opposite shore. They grounded their boat and ran to a nearby home, awakening the entire household. Everyone observed the object for some fifteen minutes before it disappeared towards the westnorthwest direction of Falcon Lake, the site of the Michalak close encounter.

The object seen on June 18 was described as oval with a rise or bubble on top. It was metallic or glassy in color. As it came towards the boat, the tree tops over which it passed glowed white. It was estimated to be 25 to 30 feet across and 15 feet thick. As it approached it was said to have an orange tinge to it. No noise was heard by anyone. An individual at a cabin near where the object was hovering was listening to his radio at the time and suddenly heard lots of interference and static. Expecting to see storm clouds which would produce this effect on his radio, he saw instead only clear sky.

DND, in co-operation with the RCMP, investigated Greene and found him to be a sincere and reliable individual with no problems related to alcohol. In fact, it was established that alcohol had not been consumed by anyone that night.

The witnesses to the event brought wilted leaves and other samples to the University of Manitoba for analysis. The federal government's Department of Forestry and Rural Development also examined the samples and the trees in the area. While fungus had caused some of the wilting, the majority of it was unexplained. The Department found that the excess wilting was perhaps due to some form of heat. The investigation was concluded, essentially with no conclusion reached.

Dr. Millman of the NRC looked into the case and dismissed the entire episode as a misidentification of the planet Venus. Unfortunately, as Hynek pointed out, no one asked if the observers saw both the object and the planet Venus at the same time. In their defense he also wondered how they could all hallucinate about the planet coming down heading for their boat, twice.

On July 3, 1967, less than a month after the Greene sighting, Warren Smith, Lorne Grovue, and fifteen-year-old Craig Dunn were 80 miles southwest of Calgary. They had been searching for the legendary Lost Lemon Mine. This is a gold mine allegedly discovered in the area in 1870 by a man named Lemon. After killing his partner he himself died without ever revealing the exact location of the mine.

At 6:30 p.m., while walking in an easterly direction, the three individuals saw an object a couple of miles away and at an altitude of about 2,000 feet. It was traveling towards them and descending. It passed in front of them and continued, disappearing behind some trees before re-emerging and hovering. Something was seen to fall from it. Warren Smith took two photographs of the object. These photos were subsequently published in the Calgary newspapers. Smith ended up sending the photos to the RCAF in Ottawa for analysis.

On November 17, 1967, Smith received a reply from Colonel W. Turner, who said the photos had been subjected to a detailed photo analysis and together with the eyewitness description the following conclusions had been reached:

The object had a diameter of some 40 to 50 feet and a depth of 11.5 to 14 feet . . . The shadow detail in the photographs showing a roll effect is more suggestive of a torus than an oblate ellipsoid. The outside surface appears to lack protrusions and highlight areas suggest a shiny, bright surface. Unfortunately, it has not been possible to identify or explain . . . the Department of National Defence and other interested agencies in UFOs have received a number of photographs of unusual aerial sightings that can neither be identified nor explained.[5]

The actual analysis report from the Defence Photographic Interpretation Centre pointed out that if the photos were faked in the darkroom, a fair knowledge of optics and photogrammetry would be required. It also stated that a similar effect could be achieved by tossing an automobile tire inner tube at 140 feet in front of the camera. One of the photos showed the object closer but behind the trees. The trees had been estimated to be 100 feet away by the witnesses.

It does not appear that Millman got involved in this case, but Hynek did. He had the photos and negatives subjected to another photographic analysis, to determine if they were fakes. The report concluded they were genuine. Warren Smith had photographed an object with a hard, silvery, and smooth surface. Hynek followed up at his own expense, with interviews of the witnesses. It was during those interviews that the three individuals signed a sworn statement to the legitimacy of the event. Hynek concluded that the three were quite credible and that the photos were believable. He stopped short of declaring or speculating as to the origin of the object.

A follow-up letter dated February 1968 from the Director of Operations states that: "The possibility exists that the object might be a secret military project . . ."[6] The report from the University of Colorado's Condon Committee also addressed this sighting. The researcher from that group concluded that there was not enough information to rule out the possibility of a hand-thrown model as mentioned in the DND report. The implication was that the witnesses could have made up the story after they developed their photos.

July 7 brought another class A incident to headquarters. The Department of Transport sent in a report that at 01:00 hrs Greenwich Mean Time (GMT) an unidentified object was picked up on radar, approximately 70 miles east of Winnipeg. Three air traffic controllers and two technicians witnessed the radar track. The object's speed had increased from 720 knots to 3,600 knots in a minute and ten seconds. All agreed the track was not due to a mechanical or electrical problem with the radar, because it tracked the object through seven sweeps. At 03:24 GMT, Kenora, Ontario, picked up an object which remained in radar contact for twenty-nine minutes. It followed Air Canada Flight 405 before disappearing, only to reappear and follow Air Canada Flight 927. Department of Transport and Department of National Defence officials were unable to account for the radar sightings.

Among the class A designations was what might well be the first report of a crop circle or crop circle–like phenomenon. These were huge, unexplained, circular patterns in farmers' fields. The vegetation — corn stalks or wheat, for example — would be flattened in strange whirls. Most such reports came from Britain in the eighties, and by the early nineties two Englishmen admitted to creating the patterns in England. They even demonstrated how it was done.

The controversy over crop circles continues, however, because England is not the only place they have been reported, and some were reported well before 1980. Patterns also began appearing in other countries, and in July 1994 a series of circles was reported in a wheat field south of Windsor, Ontario. It could be argued that these circles were made as a prank, based on the revelations in Britain. But Britain's pranksters could not have made the circles reported in 1967.

On August 8, 1967, in Duhamel, a town near Camrose, Alberta, a series of circular impressions in a pasture were reported. Local reports had it that the marks were related to the landing of one or more UFOs, since several weeks earlier, two local girls living a mile from the pasture had reported seeing a large, cream-colored UFO moving up and down a few hundred yards away from them. Mr. G. Jones of the military research establishment in Suffield was sent to investigate, along with an army photographer and a representative from headquarters.

Six circular rings were found, each making a six-inch-wide path 31 to 36 feet in diameter. The circles were only three-quarters complete and gave the appearance of having been formed by a heavy wheel moved in an almost complete circle, although no evidence was found of tire tracks or footprints entering or leaving the area. Jones' report states:

> The most striking feature of the circular marks, other than the close circularity, was they were quite distinct from the car and truck tire marks made during the week since discovery. The marks were, in general, very uniform in width and far more sharply impressed in the ground. They stood out in quite sharp contrast to the vehicle tracks in immediate proximity to them.[7]

Jones felt that the possibility of a hoax could not be ruled out but he was unable to figure out how it could have been perpetrated. The six-inch width of each circular depression was similar to that of a wheel, but if a wheel six inches wide had been used, he calculated that it would have to have been loaded to one half or three quarters of a ton and rolled in a precise circle. This could be accomplished by a wheel mounted on an arm of the appropriate radius and moved around a fixed center, but this did not seem likely as none of the circles had an indentation in the center, save for one which had a small dent in its center. Jones' other ideas included a 30-foot-long axle or a motorcycle rider turning in a circle. None seemed plausible.

He then considered the UFO solution and came up with the following calculation, based on his estimate of the pressure required on a single wheel to make the impression and presuming the load was evenly spread on a circular, narrow landing ring of metal:

> If we take the load per wheel as being 500 lb. for rough calculations, with an area of contact of four inches by two inches, this would give a loading just under 63 psi [pounds per square inch]. Reduce this down to say 50 psi, which I consider the absolute minimum needed to produce the visible marks. For simplicity, take a visible mark thirty feet in diameter and of average width five inches. This would give a total area of contact of 5400 square inches, or a total load for the UFO of 270,000 lb. This load of 135 tons would be in the right ball park for a large aircraft, presumably, a small spacecraft.[8]

The DND investigation concluded that there was no sign of radioactivity; nor was there any indication that the circles had been made by pranksters, although the possibility could not be completely excluded. There were no footprints leading into or out of the circles, even though the ground was soft from earlier rains in the area. Jones concluded with the following remark:

> The marks were sufficiently unique in my experience for me to state categorically that if I saw similar marks elsewhere

my tendency to treat the matter as a hoax would be sharply reduced. I have not, however, heard of similar markings in any previously reported UFO landings.[9]

If only reports of crop circles weren't ten to fifteen years into the future for Jones! The circles in the pasture that day were officially listed as unexplained.

On the night of October 5, 1967 (reported in the press as October 4), a rather bizarre incident made it onto the class A list. Corporal Wercicky of the RCMP and six other witnesses reported a UFO at Barrington Passage just outside of Lower Woods Harbour, Nova Scotia. The object was described as dark, greater than 60 feet, with four white lights approximately 15 feet apart. It was in view for about five minutes, traveling in an easterly direction over the water. Suddenly it descended towards the water, making a high whistling noise. It struck the water with a bright splash and looked like a single light floating on the surface. The object remained there for some time but when the RCMP officer tried approaching it by boat, it sank. The Canadian Coast Guard and a number of other boats searched the area with no success. A team of divers were dispatched as part of DND's investigation but they too found nothing. The sighting was logged as unexplained.

One week later, the October 12 edition of the *Toronto Star* carried the following related headline: "'Flying Saucers' with Coloured Lights Puzzle N.S. Village." Shag Harbour, Nova Scotia, was the scene of several strange events. Dozens of residents had reported a formation of lights in the air, over the course of several nights. On the evening of October 11, at 10:00 p.m., Lockland Cameron, his wife, daughter, brother, and his brother's wife all reported seeing an object between 500 and 600 feet off the ground and about 55 to 60 feet wide, half a mile from

Corporal Wercicky's sighting. This object had six red lights in a row and was in view for ten minutes. After the lights disappeared, four of the lights returned in a "V" or wedge formation, as they had in earlier sightings. After they disappeared again over the horizon, yellow lights were seen streaking overhead. The Camerons' television set experienced interference during the event. The Shag Harbour sightings went unexplained.

Since UFOs were proving not to be a military threat and continually defied explanation, DND officially handed over the responsibility for investigating sightings to the scientists at the National Research Council on February 16, 1968. In their letter of acceptance, the NRC stated, "Your Department should retain any reports which it is felt should be classified for reasons of military security."[10] This meant that while NRC would now be on the front line of investigating the reports and receiving the associated publicity, DND could still keep involved with some reports that the public and maybe even the NRC would never see.

Eight

The Stefan Michalak Case

"If . . . [the] reported experience were physically real, it would show the existence of alien flying vehicles in our environment."[1]

Edward U. Condon, Scientific Study of Unidentified Flying Objects, 1969

Throughout this chronology of UFO incidents, the Royal Canadian Mounted Police have figured prominently in many of the investigations, alongside the Department of National Defence. Yet the archives contain only one file in the RCMP records. It is the file on the close encounter of Stefan Michalak, revealed to this author by the RCMP archivist, and subsequently declassified in 1995. The spelling of Michalak's first name appears as it does in the RCMP file.

Stefan Michalak was born in Poland on August 7, 1916. He emigrated to Canada in 1949, after a period of military service in his home country. In the 1960s he was employed with the Inland Cement Company in Regina, Saskatchewan, as an industrial mechanic. He was later transferred with the company to Winnipeg, Manitoba. While in Saskatchewan he had studied prospecting and he furthered his studies in that field after moving to Winnipeg. It was his interest in geology and prospecting that thrust him into the UFO spotlight in May 1967. Officially, "[b]oth DND and RCMP investigation teams were unable to provide evidence which would dispute Mr. Michalak's story."[2]

On Tuesday, May 23, 1967, RCMP Corporal Davis and Constable Zacharias arrived at the Michalak home at 10:30 a.m. to take Stefan Michalak's statement. At the house was Mr. Michalak's wife, his son, Mark, and Mr. J. B. Thompson, a Canadian member of the Aerial Phenomena Research Organization (APRO), a civilian organization dedicated to the investigation of UFO incidents. The two officers interviewed Mr. Michalak for approximately two hours, during which time they reported he appeared to be suffering from an unknown illness.

Michalak told the officers that since his encounter on Saturday at Falcon Beach, he had been quite sick and unable to eat anything. He reported suffering from a constant headache and told them he believed he had lost thirteen pounds. He insisted that he had a taste of burned wiring or insulation in his mouth and that the taste seemed to somehow permeate his entire body.

Previously, Michalak had been taken to Misericordia Hospital Emergency Department for treatment of burns to his body, where he told the hospital intern the burns had been caused by the exhaust from an airplane. He did not want the intern to think he was crazy so he did not reveal what really happened.

Michalak told the RCMP his outer shirt had caught fire from

the exhaust, when he tore it off and threw it to the ground. He stamped it out after some moss caught fire from it. He also put the fire out on his undershirt, then placed it in his briefcase and brought it back home. Michalak showed the two officers the undershirt, which still reeked of burned wiring or insulation. The ski-type cap he was wearing was also burned in one area, as was one of the plastic gloves he was wearing at the time of his encounter. This glove, however, had been given to the fellow from APRO.

The following day the officers again visited Michalak, at 1:45 p.m., and interviewed him about the entire incident. He told the officers that he had been studying geology and enjoyed prospecting as a hobby. On Friday, May 19, he left work early in order to collect some things and catch a bus to his prospecting site. He packed a lunch for his next day's outing, and a magnet, raw porcelain bricks, compass, gloves, goggles, hatchet, chipping hammer, books, steel tape measure, and some notes — all the items he would need for his prospecting trip.

His son brought him to the bus, which was leaving at 7:15. His destination was Falcon Beach, about 90 miles away, east of Winnipeg near the Ontario–Manitoba border. He believes he arrived at 9:30 p.m. He then checked into a hotel/motel on the highway, read his books for an hour or an hour and a half, and then went for a coffee. He chatted briefly with the man behind the counter, asking about geologists working in the area, and then went back to his room, checked his equipment, and went to bed. At this point the RCMP officers asked specifically if he had consumed any alcoholic beverages and he replied he had not. He estimated that it was around 10:30 when he got to bed.

The next morning, May 20, he got up at 5:30 a.m. He ate some of the food he had brought with him, then left the hotel, walked up the highway a bit, turned north off the highway, and headed

into the bush. He had some familiarity with the area as he had
been there the year before. He was aiming to reach a particular
spot. On his way in he was examining rock veins when he came
upon a family of geese. They made some initial noise but then
settled down. He estimated that they were 100 to 150 feet away
from him.

Michalak continued examining the rocks and then decided to
break for lunch. It was eleven o'clock:

> After lunch I go again on my work. The geese they are mak-
> ing noise then . . . I lift my head and I look down to the
> swamp where the geese were and it hits me that a light was
> coming from over there . . . at the moment I spot one (UFO)
> another one was following after the other, there was two.
> The shape is like the sketch I made, exactly like what was in
> the air. You can't see the lines because they fit in position and
> the colors, the blue sky and the mix with red. So they whirl
> around and quit . . . It didn't make any noise at all . . . No
> noise at all. It landed and the other one stays about 10 to
> 12 feet above the ground . . . No noise at all . . .[3]

Michalak told the officers the objects had come from 255 degrees
south-southwest declination from where he was standing, as
he had checked this on his map at the time. The sky was partly
cloudy but visibility was good. There had been no sign of light-
ning in the area and it had not rained. The officers asked about
his eyesight and he stated it was good. He wore glasses only for
close work but was otherwise wearing his goggles at the time of
the sighting. He described the goggles as having one set of clear
and another set of colored lenses. He first observed the objects
through the clear lenses but later flipped over his colored lenses
because a white purplish light emanating from inside one of the

objects was hurting his eyes. His first reaction on seeing the objects was one of amazement. He was looking at both when one of them landed 100 feet away on essentially bare rock strewn with some vegetation.

The other object hovered about 10 feet off the ground before departing. It was described as being red and gray. As it began moving away, it slowly turned orange, then bright orange, then gray orange, and finally disappeared. It did not appear to be revolving although Michalak felt it was. It remained in sight for only a few minutes before leaving in the same direction it had come from. It flew away very quickly. He estimated that it was 35 to 40 feet in diameter and about 11 feet high including the dome on top.

The object that landed was initially a bright red, like hot metal, but gradually it became gray, steel gray, and then a silver kind of color. It was finally a pale brass yellow with a very smooth finish. As it was settling down a whirling or whistling noise was heard, like a small motor. Michalak could also feel the air, as if it were being sucked up somehow as the craft rested on the ground, and there was a suction-like sound. No engine noise was heard. It sat on the ground for a good forty-five minutes, but after about ten minutes a hatch opened.

He saw a column of bright violet light which appeared to be coming from underneath the top of the dome. The walls of the object were between 18 and 20 or 22 inches thick, with ribs inside the walls. It was at this point that he began approaching the object.

When I started going I hear a noise. There was positive human being talking in there . . . Men . . . But the first idea ever comes to me was Americans. So I say well, if you are Yankee boys, you come out and don't be afraid. I say I don't sell your secret for a lousy green buck, if you need help just

come out. Then the voice stopped. Completely . . . I think
it was maybe two, three times exchanging short conversation. And that was it. They never say a word after . . . Then
I say in German and Italian . . .[4]

Michalak explained how he continued calling out in various lan-
guages including Polish, Ukrainian, and Russian but to no avail.

As he continued trying to communicate, the hatch closed
quickly: "The closing was a one plate moving horizontally and
another one horizontally in the other direction and the third one
was pushed out . . . It was very well-fitted."[5]

As he got closer to the object, Michalak said he could see and
feel the heat radiating from it. The various colors of the metal
indicated that the surface was hot. It then began turning red and
started to rotate counterclockwise. He did not hear any engines
start but there was an increasing whirring sound. As it turned
he found himself facing some sort of grillwork arrangement. He
reached out with his gloved hand and touched beside the grillwork. The plastic of the glove began to melt and so he removed
his hand.

As the object started to take off, a blast of hot air came from the
grillwork. Michalak spun to the ground, his shirt on fire. He ripped
his shirt off and then his undershirt and turned round just in time
to see the craft leave at a fantastic rate of speed. He noted that it
did not take off straight into the air but rather tipped a little and
actually left at an angle. He said there was no noise like a jet but
that it moved much faster than any jet, perhaps three or four
times faster. As it departed it turned quite red and then gradually
it changed to orange before disappearing into the clouds. A few
minutes later conventional aircraft were seen passing overhead.

The officers asked him how far he was from the nearest power
lines. His estimate was about two miles. He was asked about his

shirt again and he reiterated how he tore off his outer shirt and stamped out the fire. He was concerned about starting a forest fire. He left the shirt there, where he stamped it out. He then walked around for a while and recalls seeing an area of blown-out vegetation and a circular area about 10 feet in diameter. He was asked if he left anything else besides his shirt and he replied he had left his steel tape measure. He also noted that on the way in he had found an old saw which he left on a rock.

After the craft departed he remained at the site for about ten minutes before heading out for the highway. At that point he started feeling nauseous and began to vomit. He vomited again and finally, as he reached the highway, he vomited again and again, repeatedly for two minutes. While observing the craft on the ground, he had noticed the intense smell of burning electrical wires or insulation. This smell now seemed to be emanating from his body and he could taste it in his mouth. Since the incident, he reported he had not been able to eat anything and was still feeling quite ill, experiencing headaches and blackouts. He estimated that he was losing five pounds a day.

When he reached the highway, he was able to flag down a passing Falcon Beach Highway Patrol car. Constable G.A. Solotki was driving in the car when he saw Michalak flagging him down about 3:00 p.m. on the afternoon of Saturday, May 20. This was on the Trans-Canada Highway, about half a mile west of the Falcon Beach entrance. Solotki had initially passed by him but turned back when he realized Michalak was waving frantically at him. Constable Solotki's classified report stated that Michalak was very excited. Michalak told him he was in the bush prospecting and claimed he had just seen two spaceships. At Solotki's request, he drew a diagram of the vehicle as a saucer shape. (Presumably, because of the speed at departure, Michalak had decided they were not man-made, and he had also been aware of flying saucers from media reports.) They were glowing red and rotating. He had touched one of them and got burned. He had also burned his hat and shirt and showed his hat to the constable, but refused to show his shirt, claiming that he wanted no publicity. His eyes were red and bloodshot and he was acting in an irrational manner, prompting Solotki to believe that he had been on a drinking binge and was now having a hangover. However, there was no smell of alcohol on him.

Each time Solotki tried to approach, Michalak backed off and became unco-operative. All he had with him was a briefcase and he claimed the burnt shirt was inside. Although he had said he was prospecting, he had no camping equipment, but he explained he had arrived by bus on Friday. He refused to show Solotki the location of the landing site but did show him that he had received burns to his chest, which Solotki said looked as though he was "rubbing ash onto the skin."[6] Solotki also noticed a burn on Michalak's hat but saw no marks on his head. The constable then asked if he could give Michalak a lift back to Falcon Beach, where medical treatment could be arranged. Michalak refused, claiming he was alright. The constable then left and Michalak made his own way back to the hotel. Other versions of this meeting with Solotki have him telling Michalak that he had other duties and abruptly leaving him standing by the roadside. Solotki's report is significant because it shows that something unusual did happen to Michalak, given his condition at the time.

According to Solotki's report, half an hour later Michalak arrived at the police detachment office. Constable L. A. Schmalz had discovered that in the interim Michalak had asked the hotel owner's wife where he could find a doctor. She replied that he should see the RCMP if something was wrong since a doctor would not be available until July 1. This is when he went to the RCMP office. He asked for Solotki but refused to enter the office.

Wilbert B. Smith, Canadian Department of Transport.
— *The Arthur Bray Collection, University of Ottawa*

Dr. Omond Solandt, chairman of the Canadian Defence Research Board.
— *Department of National Defence* CF-66-395

Dr. Vannevar Bush, chairman of the Joint Research and Development Board of the National Military Establishment.
— *The MIT Museum*

The Right Honourable Brooke Claxton, Minister of National Defence.
— *National Archives of Canada* C-071164

Artist's rendering of several Avrocars in flight.
— *U.S. Army Transportation Museum, Fort Eustis, Virginia*

Official USAF press release photo of the Avrocar.
— *National Archives of Canada* PA-194835

Avro flight test pilot "Spud" Potocki takes the Avrocar up for a spin.
— *U.S. Army Transportation Museum, Fort Eustis, Virginia*

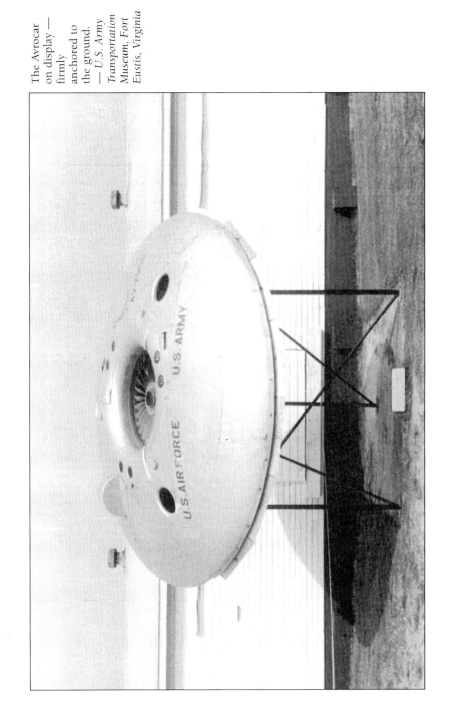

The Avrocar on display — firmly anchored to the ground.
— *U.S. Army Transportation Museum, Fort Eustis, Virginia*

Stefan Michalak standing at the spot where he alleges to have touched the UFO.
— *National Archives of Canada C-143793*

Fifteen-foot-diameter circular imprint at the Michalak landing site, made "by a force as made by air at very high velocity." Square box indicates where radioactive material was found.
— *National Archives of Canada C-143794*

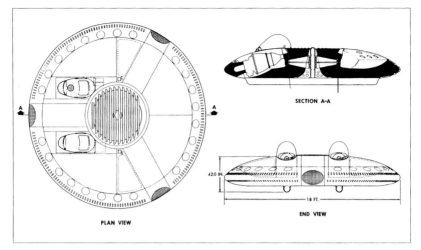

PLAN VIEW

SECTION A-A

END VIEW

42.0 IN

18 FT.

Avrocar profiles show grillwork strikingly similar to the one that left its mark on
Stefan Michalak. Could he have encountered a made-in-Canada UFO?
— *Department of National Defence 57-17033*

Fig. 3 Three-View General Arrangement of Research Aircraft
(Radial Flow Engine)

Profiles of Project Silver Bug: the USAF's version of Avro's supersonic Project Y2.
— *Air Technical Intelligence Center T55-2049*

He spoke to the constable outside and asked where he might get medical attention. He was advised that the nearest doctors were in Kenora, Ontario, or Steinbach, Manitoba. He again asked Solotki not to tell anyone about his incident as he wanted no publicity and told him he was going to catch the 8:10 p.m. bus to Winnipeg. The last time he was seen by the constable was near the hotel, waiting for the bus. Here again, other versions of the story have Michalak waiting outside the hotel coffee shop and finally asking someone in the coffee shop if a doctor was available. The RCMP are painted as unco-operative, but this is sharply contradicted by Solotki's report.

Michalak essentially corroborated Solotki's version of events to the two officers who were now in his home. He added that he had not wished to show Solotki his shirt because he was afraid the object was radioactive and did not want to contaminate him. This is also why he backed away from Solotki several times. He was reluctant to show Solotki the landing site because he said he had found a nickel strike and wanted to keep the location hidden until he could file a claim. He did say that he would eventually take the RCMP to the site.

One thing puzzled the two interviewing officers at his home. Michalak had told Solotki he wanted no publicity, presumably to keep the location of his site secret. When Michalak returned to the hotel, however, he decided he needed medical attention but instead he called the *Winnipeg Tribune*. He told the officers he felt that the *Tribune* could help him with his medical problem somehow but, for someone who had insisted he wanted no publicity, his actions were ill-advised. He waited several hours at the hotel, then boarded a bus and headed back to Winnipeg on Saturday night, where his son picked him up and brought him to the hospital.

In order to establish some form of credibility, the RCMP did a background check on Michalak. His employer described him as a good and trusted employee. Inquiries were also made at the

Selkirk Mental Hospital, the Brandon Mental Hospital, and the Winnipeg Psychiatric Institute in an effort to determine if there had been any history of mental disturbance. There was no evidence of this. None of Michalak's associates and co-workers had noticed anything unusual about his behavior which might indicate the onset of a mental problem. In short, Michalak checked out.

At his initial interview with the two officers, Michalak had shown them the burn mark on his abdomen. It was described by the officers as:

> . . . a large burn that covers an area approximately 1 foot in diameter . . . blotchy and with unburned areas inside the burned perimeter area. There was no indication of blistering. It resembled an exceptionally severe sunburn in the one spot. Michalak was very uncomfortable while we were speaking to him and reminded me of a person that had come out of an epileptic fit . . . his head was aching so badly that it pained him to move . . .[7]

Michalak also indicated that he had been examined by his own physician, Dr. R. Douglas Oatway. The officers spoke with Oatway on the afternoon of May 23. Oatway could not find anything mentally wrong with Michalak, but noted that he had been through an ordeal of some kind. As with the hospital intern, Michalak had not made his doctor aware of the circumstances of the incident during his examination. What Oatway found was:

> . . . an area of first degree burns over the upper abdomen, covering an area 7–8 inches and consisting of several round irregular shaped burns the size of a silver dollar or less. These were a dull red in color, the hair over the lower chest was singed as was the hair on the forehead with some questionable redness on the right cheek and temple.[8]

The burns in fact resembled the grillwork pattern from which the blast emanated. Oatway also had the undershirt, hat, and blood checked for radioactivity at the Winnipeg Cancer Research Institute. All had come back negative. He was trying to determine why Michalak had lost his appetite and was unable to keep any food down, but Oatway found nothing. He also gave him medicine for the headaches and sedatives to keep him calm. Michalak would later be examined at the Mayo Clinic, again with no satisfactory explanation as to the cause of his illness.

On May 25 the RCMP decided to try and find the landing site, even though Oatway recommended that Michalak was not yet able to accompany them. Michalak provided some general directions and with the help of the RCAF the two interviewing officers and seven military members set off by helicopter to find the spot. On the way into the bush, the group found the old saw that Michalak had said he placed on a rock. They also found a shopping bag Michalak had thrown away. The actual landing site, however, eluded them.

It was decided to wait until Michalak was well enough to join the search party before making another attempt. Arrangements were also made with Investigating Officer Squadron Leader P. Bissky of the RCAF. He would be called in when Michalak was ready to join the group. Bissky wanted to find out if there was any radioactivity in the area of the landing site.

On May 30 Bissky and RCMP Corporal Davis approached Michalak about finding the landing site. Michalak was still not well enough to go with them but provided more details and even drew a sketch of the terrain. He said there was a flat piece of rock, 300 feet long by 100 feet wide, where the landing had occurred. Corporal Davis noted that such large areas of rock were rare, increasing the chances of finding it. The following day a search was conducted since Corporal Davis reasoned that if they waited much longer, the landing site would become difficult to find because of the surrounding plant growth.

Squadron Leader Bissky had arranged for a military helicopter and he and Davis went up. Other RCAF and RCMP personnel searched on foot. They continued until dark before calling it off. Nothing had been found so it was decided to try and get Michalak to be on hand for the next try. That evening Davis and RCMP Constable Anderson visited Michalak. This time Michalak said he was ready and arrangements were made to pick him up the next morning, June 1.

Michalak accompanied Corporal Davis in the helicopter. Unfortunately, though, because the area looked so much different from the air, Michalak was unable to recognize any landmarks. In the afternoon he was taken on foot to where the saw and shopping bag had been found, in the hope that he would remember the rest of the way in to the landing site. Approximately three or four miles of terrain were covered while Michalak seemed to be wandering aimlessly. He told the others that on his prospecting forays into the forest, he would look for and follow quartz veins. He would not pay attention to the surrounding areas or specific landmarks. Once he felt he had done enough prospecting, he would check his compass and find his way out again. This was why he could now not find the site.

As the search progressed on foot, Bissky took to the air, looking for spots resembling Michalak's descriptions. None of them proved to be the site and Michalak was quite upset with himself for not being able to find it. He was returned home to Winnipeg around 10:00 p.m. The following day the search resumed by helicopter only, without Michalak, but by noon it was called off.

While the searches for the landing site were being initiated, Constable Schmalz was checking out another aspect of the story. Michalak had said that he did not consume any alcohol the night before; he had some coffee, spoke to the man behind the counter, and then went to his room. Constable Schmalz checked with hotel staff. William Hastings was tending bar until 8:00 p.m. that night and saw no one resembling Michalak. Then James Davidson, the manager of the lounge and dining room, took over. He told Schmalz that he served Michalak three bottles of beer by 9:30 p.m., after which Michalak left the bar. He returned at 11:00 p.m. and consumed two more bottles in the dining room. Davidson said Michalak asked him about other prospectors in the area and looked as though he was feeling the effects from the alcohol. Davidson said Michalak seemed sure about finding something in the bush the following day.

It was pointed out to Davidson that he could not have served Michalak between 8:00 and 9:30 p.m. because the bus from Winnipeg did not get in until 9:15 or 9:30 p.m. Davidson agreed that he might have gotten the time wrong but insisted that it was Michalak he served. Davidson recognized him on June 1, the day he was brought out to help in the search. Michalak on the other hand remained steadfast that he did not consume any alcohol.

One other check was made. The maid who cleaned Michalak's room the following morning was also asked if she had found any evidence of alcohol in the room, but she had not. Liquor purchase receipts at both the hotel and the liquor store were checked to determine if Michalak had purchased any liquor to take out. The results were negative.

By now the story had been circulating in the press and caught the attention of the Condon Committee at the University of Colorado. Dr. Roy Craig was sent to interview Michalak. The DND file notes that Craig, Mr. Thompson from APRO, two *Life* magazine photographers, and Michalak actually tried to locate the site on May 29. The RCMP report, however, indicates that this attempt was made on Sunday, June 4. The reason for the discrepancy is unclear but subsequent information points to the RCMP report as the accurate one. The Condon Committee's report itself does not give a date.

According to the RCMP report, Craig was initially very impressed with the story when he interviewed Michalak on June 3. After wandering aimlessly in the bush with Michalak looking for the landing site on June 4, Craig began to doubt the story. He visited Bissky on June 5 and told him the search had to be abandoned as Michalak was going around in circles. There were also some discrepancies as to what the actual site looked like, as described to Craig and to Bissky and the RCMP. Craig thought that Michalak had perhaps hallucinated the whole thing and that his family was now enjoying the attention and publicity of it all. Both Bissky and Craig noted the continued presence of Barry Thompson of the APRO organization and thought there appeared to be some monetary-gain aspects to the relationship.

The burns to Michalak's body were puzzling, however, and were definitely not a hallucination. Bissky attempted to find out if Michalak had accidentally encountered high-tension wires or something similar that could have caused his injuries. There were no power lines in the area but a microwave tower nearby was checked out. A burnt shirt was found near the tower but proved to be a cleaning rag used by telephone personnel during tower renovations. The source of the burns and Michalak's sickness remained unexplained.

On June 26 Michalak called Bissky and told him that on June 24 he again went looking for the site. This time he was accompanied by a Mr. G. Hart. Although some accounts have listed Hart as a personal friend, the DND and RCMP records indicate that Michalak had told them Hart was in fact a stranger, having called him once before and advised him he could use a cottage at Falcon Lake the next time he decided to look for the landing site.

On the morning of Sunday, June 25, Hart and Michalak found the site. Michalak took some photos and retrieved the remnants of his outer shirt, along with some samples of dirt and moss. A 15-foot circular outline was still noticeable. During this trip Michalak also found the ore he was looking for but again refused to disclose the location of the site to others. He remained adamant about not disclosing the location for fear of others jumping his claim. After he filed his claim, he discovered that it had to be shared with Hart, the man he was with at the time of the find.

Corporal Davis noted in his report that Michalak had originally stated he wanted to show the RCMP the site but was now reluctant. More importantly, Michalak had been advised that if he should find the site, he should not remove anything from it until the RCMP or the RCAF had a chance to investigate. Instead of following these instructions, Michalak removed several items.

On the evening of June 26, Bissky went to see Michalak. Constable Anderson accompanied Bissky since Corporal Davis was unable to. Michalak was quite distressed to see the constable and wanted to know how the RCMP had found out that he had discovered the landing site. He was reminded that Corporal Davis had asked him to contact the RCMP should he find the site. Michalak denied knowing of this request and said he was upset at all the background checks the RCMP had conducted on him. In any event, Michalak brought Bissky to his basement where he brought out a plastic bag with dirt and what looked like pieces of a burnt green shirt for him to send to Ottawa for analysis, and a steel measuring tape.

On July 24 the test results on the sample were returned, but not to Bissky. They were sent instead to Corporal Davis, who was unaware that the samples had been sent for analysis and was confused when he received the results. After requesting clarification, he was advised that the Defence Research Board lab in Ottawa had sent the samples to the Radiation Protection Division of the Ministry of Health and Welfare. Corporal Davis notified Bissky, who had been away on holiday.

Bissky was surprised that the results were sent to the RCMP and not to the RCAF since he was the one who had sent the samples. Why the mix-up occurred is not entirely clear. In any event, the samples were found to be highly radioactive — 0.5 microcuries of radium 226 — and Bissky advised Corporal Davis by message that since these samples had come from a larger portion held by Michalak, the balance might also be contaminated. The message to the RCMP also stated that a radiation expert, Stuart Hunt, was going to travel to Winnipeg to investigate the situation. Davis believed that Hunt would be successful in persuading Michalak to reveal the landing site's location, in light of the potential danger from the radioactivity.

On July 26 Hunt, Davis, Bissky, and a representative from the Manitoba Department of Health, Mr. D. Thompson, visited Michalak. They examined the samples in his basement and found them to be radioactive. They also noted that Michalak handled them with his bare hands and seemingly had little concern about being exposed. They learned that Michalak had in fact given samples and shown the landing site on July 17 to Barry Thompson of APRO and that *Life* magazine photographers had taken photos of the site.

On July 27 Michalak finally took the RCMP and the RCAF to the landing site. It took forty-five minutes to reach from the Falcon Beach Hotel. The site was about two and a half miles north of the highway. Michalak was now very co-operative with all concerned and no longer seemed to harbor any suspicions about the RCMP. The site proved to be about 50 yards from where the first search with Michalak had taken place but was behind a heavy thicket of trees and brush, in a ravine. Michalak said he might have been able to find it during the earlier attempt if he had been left alone, without so many people continually suggesting places for him to look.

The area did have some resemblance to the sketches that Michalak had drawn earlier but it was much smaller than originally thought. There was no clearing or opening to the southwest as previously indicated by Michalak and so it had been ignored in earlier searches as a potential site. There was no evidence other than a semicircle of 15-foot diameter on the rock face, where the moss had been removed. The rest of the circle could be seen except for a small portion which was not present due to a depression in the rock itself. The circle was carefully examined and there appeared to be no indication that the moss had been manually removed in some way, although this could not be completely ruled out. Bissky noted that the moss seemed to have been cleared "by a force such as made by air at very high velocity." [9]

Near the circle, in an area where there was no moss, was where Michalak claimed to have stood when he touched the craft. Unfortunately there were no traces of his burned shirt, as he must have picked it all up when he found the site with Hart. The spot where Michalak was chipping the rock when he first saw the object was about 200 feet south. The area between the trees from which the two objects came and left was at 20 degrees north by northeast, not 255 degrees south by southwest as he had originally reported. Michalak now claims he must have just made a mistake.

Hunt took readings of radioactivity around the site but found some only in a crack in the rock. He said it was a small quantity and therefore did not pose a health hazard to the general public. The radioactive material was radium 226, a substance used commercially and also as a discharge from nuclear reactors. In his own report, Hunt noted that the entire area of contamination was about 100 square inches. He also felt that the origin of the circular outline was debatable, seeming somewhat more skeptical than the RCMP investigators.

Hunt had the samples from Michalak's home and those from the site examined by the Environmental Sanitation Laboratory. Those from the site gave an indication that they were contaminated with radium-luminous paint but those from Michalak did not. Hunt tried to locate the origin of the contamination and examined a burial ground for radium, but it had not been disturbed. A check was also made of the Inland Cement Company to determine if they used or were in possession of radioactive sources. This too proved negative.

A further check was made with Plaxlab Products Limited, the advertising firm with which Barry Thompson was associated. Plaxlab did not use radioactive materials, although Thompson had taken some soil samples to the nuclear medicine department of the Winnipeg General Hospital, where they detected a 1.4-MeV (mega–electron volt) energy peak according to him. This has been reported elsewhere as a 190-keV peak but remains consistent with levels of natural occurrence. A check with the hospital revealed that they detected radioactivity in the samples. They also examined Michalak's burns but found them to be thermal in nature and not related to radioactivity. Of the samples in Thompson's possession, those obtained directly from the site showed levels of 1 mR/hr (milli-Roentgens per hour, a measure of exposure rate). Hunt never was able to find the source of the contamination and concluded that levels were not high enough to cause any kind of hazard to the public.

The RCMP summarized their report by noting that their expert did not believe luminous paint was the source of the radioactivity as it was no longer in great use. As for the whole incident, several discrepancies and other problems were noted: the five bottles of beer which the bartender claimed he served to Michalak and which the latter denied; Michalak's inability to find the landing site; the error in the direction that the two objects left the scene even though he originally claimed to have checked it with his compass and a map; his willingness to confide in a complete stranger, G. Hart, after saying he wanted no outsiders involved in order to protect his claims; and finally, Michalak's removal of the items from the landing site and his denial that the RCMP had asked him to leave the site undisturbed should he find it.

On the other hand, there were several unexplained elements: his illness, including headaches and weight loss, fluctuations in his blood cell count, the burns to his body and clothing, the circle in the rock at the landing site, and his state of agitation shortly after the incident, when he encountered Solotki on the highway. The RCMP report stated:

> Our investigation has not been able to resolve any of these points mentioned and we have not been able to account for the inconsistent actions of Michalak . . . our file is being terminated."[10]

Bissky essentially agreed with the RCMP report. He noted, however, that torrential rains on July 17 probably destroyed any remaining evidence that might have existed at the site. He gave a description of the photos of the site taken by the RCMP and noted some additional discrepancies not cited in the RCMP report. He stated that given the alleged size of the object (35 to 40 feet), there should have been damage to the surrounding tree tops, but none was found.

Bissky also wrote that it was proven that Michalak did like to consume alcoholic beverages. Back at the hotel after the search, he had consumed rye and ginger ale but had refused beer. This prompted Bissky to speculate that perhaps what Michalak experienced was a hallucination brought on by a drinking binge the night before, but the RCMP had found no evidence of this. Also, Michalak had told the RCMP that at most he would have had a glass of wine if anything because he preferred this to beer. Therefore, that he refused beer later simply adds to his claim he did not drink beer the night in question. The removal of all evidence from the site disturbed Bissky, as it did the RCMP. Even Bissky, though, conceded that the illness, the burns, and the circle were inexplicable. The overall conclusion was that neither the RCMP nor the RCAF were able to find any evidence to dispute Michalak's story.

For their part, Craig and the Condon Committee noted that near the site was a watchtower, with six other towers in the distance. Forest rangers who were interviewed said that because the forest was dry, the burning shirt could have caused a forest fire, and the watchmen in the towers would have seen the small fire and the objects coming and going. There is no indication that any of the watchmen in the tower that day were contacted.

Craig's report also noted that a golf course lies in the direction of departure given by Michalak but that no golfers reported anything unusual. But as noted in the RCMP report, a copy of which the Condon Committee possessed, Michalak had originally been completely wrong about the direction of departure, so the craft would not have overflown the golfers. The final conclusion noted the remaining inconsistencies and stated simply that the incident did not provide evidence that an unconventional craft had been seen. There was no comment concerning the illness and burns.

Subsequent writings on the Michalak case have been relatively accurate, but there have been some discrepancies in the retelling. For example, it has been written that Michalak's hat brushed the side of the craft and got burnt and that his glove was melted when he reached out and touched the side of the craft. In fact, the hat did not brush the craft, and Michalak touched an area near the grillwork which one might expect to be hot if it were an exhaust port. Also, it has been said that the RCMP officer who was flagged down by Michalak simply listened to his story but offered no assistance. In fact, the officer offered assistance, according to his police report, but was refused.

Requests to Parliament for all existing records on the case were made on at least four separate occasions but each time the government refused to turn over any files, fueling speculation that a cover-up was underway. The RCMP file that was declassified in 1995 contained the names and addresses of individuals who had been approached by the RCMP with respect to the sighting and Michalak himself. On declassification, their specific personal comments about Michalak were duly excised. It is possible that the reason for the secrecy was simply to protect the privacy of the individuals who had been queried and perhaps to protect Michalak himself. There may have also been some concern that police procedures would have been compromised. If anything, the file certainly appears to treat the matter objectively and corroborates information held in the DND file, which was also recently declassified. While noting the discrepancies in his story, both files support the conclusion that something which cannot be explained happened. In hindsight, it probably would have been better to have released the files at the time they were first requested, especially since Michalak himself had gone public with his story.

A year after the incident, Michalak returned to the site and found two silver bars under the lichen on the rock where the object had hovered. The bars were radioactive, but what cannot be explained is why they had been missed by Health and Welfare and other researchers who had returned to the site on several occasions — unless of course the bars had just been planted there. It is felt that this find has actually detracted from the credibility of the whole story rather than adding to it.

In the early nineties Stefan Michalak was profiled on a television documentary. He still bore the burn marks to his body and stuck to his story about what he saw.

On January 3, 1997, the Michalak case was one of four discussed during a telecast by the Arts & Entertainment Network of a program called *The Unexplained*. Michalak's son maintained that his father did not make up the story.

A review of the Michalak case leaves one to wonder, was it all just a hoax as Dr. Craig believed, a hoax fabricated to hide something else that was going on, a hallucination, or a real UFO close encounter? If it were not for the burns to his body, the entire story might have been dismissed outright. The suggestion is that something extraordinary did indeed happen to Stefan Michalak on that Saturday afternoon, but the question remains: what?

If we assume that Michalak's claims are honest, and there is no reason to assume otherwise despite some minor discrepancies, the following picture emerges. The description of the vehicles, the grillwork, the electrical smell, the angular takeoff, the blast of exhaust, and the human-sounding voices all suggest that what was seen was a man-made object rather than something extraterrestrial. There was no missing time or telepathic communication as reported in numerous other incidents (including the famous Betty and Barney Hill abduction case of 1961), no feeling of weightlessness, no incredible zig-zag or angular turns in the flight of the vehicles, no dreams, nor any of the other effects commonly reported with such encounters. These were all effects that were known at the time and which Michalak might have been aware of since he admitted to having read about UFO accounts, yet they did not form part of his story. Their absence tends to add a certain air of credibility to his story, since it would have been simpler to borrow details from those other accounts.

By Michalak's own account, his initial immediate reaction was that these objects were probably American secret craft, and he believed this even more when he heard the human-sounding voices. It should be noted that if these voices were emanating from within the craft, and if there was any accent in the voices, then even if they were speaking English, it might have sounded like an unrecognizable but human language. If it was a secret craft, the people inside would definitely not have responded, and they would have taken off precisely as they did.

Radioactivity seems always to be considered a sign of extraterrestrial presence, yet there is no logical reason for this. One might expect the radioactivity to have been from the craft's propulsion system, but UFO propulsion is generally associated with some sort of magnetic, electromagnetic, or matter/antimatter source, not radioactive nuclear phenomena. If anything, radioactivity would indicate a propulsive mechanism built on earth, using conventional though experimental means such as a fission reaction. But even today, experiments to develop nuclear fusion, which leaves no radioactivity, are ongoing. A superior race capable of interstellar travel would presumably have conquered the nuclear fusion problem.

The radioactivity found at the landing site was most likely naturally occurring or might have been planted as was being suggested by Hunt. On the other hand, if it was caused by some form of leakage or residue from the object, it would indicate that the craft was man-made. Could Michalak have seen an experimental model of the so-called atomic-powered aircraft which was to have been revealed back in 1950–51? Or perhaps he saw a follow-on to the Avrocar with a new type of engine. After all, the Avrocar was supposedly ready for supersonic flight when it was terminated in Canada. Perhaps the United States had developed it into a working prototype.

Then there is the statement made by the Canadian Secretary of the Defence Staff, Commodore F. B. Caldwell. He was commenting in a letter written in 1968 about the Warren Smith sighting of 1967 and the two photographs taken by Smith. Rather than say the sighting was unexplained or that the pictures might have been faked by throwing a model or a tire in front of the lenses, as did the Condon report, he said, "The possibility exists that the object might be a secret military project . . ."[11] That conclusion prompts the question, what were secret military projects doing flying around the wilds of Ontario and Manitoba? In fact, it is not unusual for such tests to be conducted in remote areas, presumably away from potential witnesses. Also, the Canadian landscape mimics that of other countries, as well as the lunar surface. Cruise missiles have been tested there because of this, and Apollo lunar astronauts have been trained in the Canadian wilds.

Writing in *The Roswell Incident*, authors Berlitz and Moore tell the story of a sergeant who, on befriending a fighter pilot while on duty at Edwards Air Force Base, was taken to a particular hangar. Once inside, the sergeant was allowed a glimpse behind a heavy curtain. He claims he saw a circular craft perhaps 25 to 30 feet in diameter, with a dome on top. He was told that such craft were being test-flown by the USAF. The incident allegedly occurred in 1967.

One person who believes that Project Y, or something like it, was in fact made a reality is Major George A. Filer, USAF (retired). In 1962 Filer was in a tanker aircraft over the North Sea. His aircraft had just completed a night refueling operation when London Control asked if they could investigate an unidentified flying object that was being picked up on radar. Other traffic was cleared and the tanker was requested to proceed towards the Oxford, Stonehenge area. The object was picked up on the aircraft's radar at the one o'clock position and appeared to be hovering. As the aircraft dropped to 1,000 feet and closed to within a mile, Filer was able to see the UFO. It was circular and bright. He saw its lights as it shot straight up like a rocket, moving at over 1,000 miles an hour. London Control radioed that no rockets were being launched from that part of England. The incident was not reported, partly because of the stigma associated with such reports in those days but also because Filer believed that what he saw was man-made.

It has been asked, if this kind of technology is available, why continue to build conventional aircraft?

Jack Pickett was told that the designs for the craft he had seen had been shelved due to the availability of more practical designs, i.e., normal airplanes. The reason usually given is the maneuverability problems of the circular aircraft. When one develops a new aircraft, taking off and landing are not the only considerations. One must look at the maneuverability, the range, the reliability over time, the ease of repair, and whether the aircraft will satisfy the proposed mission. Therefore, even if vertical take-off and hovering is achieved, the other factors may rule against immediate production and replacement of conventional designs. There is also the economic impact of suddenly putting a host of aircraft companies out of business with a successful, radical concept. For an example, one has only to look at the Stealth Fighter. It has not replaced all existing conventional aircraft.

Did Michalak see an experimental man-made craft? The description and circumstances certainly lean in favor of this, rather than an extraterrestrial flying saucer.

Nine

Into the Present

"We know so little about the vast universe, poised as we are on our tiny vantage point, the earth, that things far beyond our imagination may indeed be possible."[1]

Dr. Allen J. Hynek, USAF UFO investigator, 1977

Canada's Department of National Defence was still very much involved in UFO sightings in the 1970s, as the following episode demonstrates. The *National Enquirer's* headline for August 1976 screamed, "Air Defense Chiefs Admit: We Tracked UFO on Radar and Scrambled Fighter Jets to Intercept." The tabloid told the story of what had happened eight months earlier, on the night of November 11, 1975.

The *Enquirer* article was essentially correct. Witnesses included police officers, military personnel at the NORAD radar base in

Falconbridge, Ontario, and numerous civilians. It was one of the few incidents to include simultaneous radar, visual, and photographic evidence.

Reports of strange lights were called in to police headquarters at about 3:00 a.m. by people in Sudbury, Ontario, some 15 miles southwest of the Falconbridge radar site. The lights were low in the sky but suddenly shot straight up. Two police officers saw four objects, three of which appeared to be hovering while the fourth was moving in a kind of circular motion. Two other officers spotted an object through binoculars. They said it was shaped like a cylinder and they observed it until 7:00 a.m. Other officers also reported bright objects.

At the Falconbridge radar station the commanding officer, Major Robert Oliver, and five others saw three objects. These objects were observed through binoculars but no identification could be made. Oliver advised the *Enquirer* that he believed both DND and the U.S. authorities investigated the more serious reports like this one.

Two jets were finally scrambled from Selfridge Air Force Base in Detroit, Michigan, at about 10:45 a.m. These jets found nothing. Captain Gordon Hilchie, Director of Public Affairs for the 22nd NORAD Region Control Centre at North Bay, stated that the objects were tracked 25 to 30 miles south of the radar site at Falconbridge. They shot up from 26,000 feet to 45,000 feet, stopped for a period of time, and then shot up to 72,000 feet.

The North Bay *Nugget* also reported the sighting and included a photograph taken by a staff photographer. Colonel G. W. Patterson, Chief of Staff of Operations for the Air Defence Group and Deputy Commander of Operations for the 22nd NORAD Region Control Centre, was interviewed, along with Lieutenant Colonel B. Wooding, Director of the 22nd NORAD Region Control Centre. They were asked why radar doesn't always pick up UFOs. Wooding explained that many factors come into play. For example, if the object is too low, or is moving too quickly or too slowly, it may be missed. If it is constructed out of non-metallic material or material that absorbs a radar signal rather than reflecting it back, the object will go unnoticed. Also, radar is tuned to specific frequencies. Search radar is designed to look for aircraft while height-finder radar is designed to determine the height of objects. In addition, radar can be fooled by flocks of birds or temperature effects, which can mask a UFO or appear as a trace which might be interpreted as a UFO. This could explain why not all the radar installations picked up the objects over Sudbury and that those that did might have been fooled.

In his book, *Skunk Works*, Ben Rich reveals some of the secrets behind stealth technology and the Stealth Fighter. His revelations provide another reason why flying saucers cannot always be detected on radar. He notes that the flying saucer shape is practically the ultimate in low observability. That is, due simply to a saucer's shape, the laws of physics make the craft difficult to detect on radar. Rich adds that his crew at the Skunk Works wished they could build one. The Skunk Works, for the uninitiated, was the name given to Lockheed Martin's covert design and development section. It developed many black programs secretly funded under the guise of other names and other programs.

As for the visual sightings in Sudbury, Patterson added that strange atmospheric effects could have caused the illusion of UFOs in a way similar to the effects of the Northern Lights. He also mentioned effects from lenticular clouds, which can sometimes magnify bright stars or planets. Ian Halliday of the National Research Council was consulted and noted that the effects observed could have been due to unusual atmospheric phenomena. Observers might even have been watching aircraft but heard no sound due to atmospheric effects which would carry the sound upwards and away from the ground. Halliday also spoke of how the planets might be misinterpreted under certain conditions, and finally said that observers estimating distances and heights could easily be mistaken, if they had no point of reference.

In 1995 a file marked "Secret" was declassified for this author. It contains pages from the 22nd NORAD Region Air Traffic Control Log Book, which gives a blow-by-blow account of what was reported that morning in 1975. The log book corroborates the stories in the papers and contains a few extra noteworthy details. All times are given in Greenwich Mean Time (GMT), as recorded in the file.

On November 11, at 10:43 GMT, the 22nd NORAD Region Control Centre received a call about two UFOs being chased by the Sudbury police. Was air traffic control picking them up on radar? At 11:18 GMT Canadian Forces Base Falconbridge called about a UFO over the base and another one reportedly over the Ontario Provincial Police building in downtown Sudbury. The UFO over the base was described as resembling a gem with colored lights around it.

At 11:47 Major Oliver from Falconbridge called in. He stated that between 11:15 and 11:29 GMT he saw two UFOs with brilliant lights. One was at 200 degrees from Falconbridge and the other at 180 degrees and much further away. Not reported in the press was that Oliver took three snapshots with a brownie camera. It is not known what became of those photographs or whether they even turned out. He also observed the closer object through binoculars. It was "rising vertically at tremendous speed . . ."[2] The height-finder radar picked it up first at 44,000 feet and then at 72,000 feet. This means that the altitudes were not guessed by the observers, as had been reported in the media, but were in fact recorded by the radar. The object was described as being circular, well lighted, and with two black spots in the center. By 13:24 GMT, radio station CKSO called requesting information about the UFOs but was given no comment as to any specific details at that time.

At 17:27 GMT Patterson, who was at NORAD Headquarters in Colorado, was advised that the object was still in view and that Selfridge Air Force Base had been notified. At 17:50 GMT two F-106 aircraft from the American base were scrambled. At 18:53 they reported that searches had been made from 8,000 to 30,000 feet with no contact with any objects.

At 07:10 GMT on November 12, Master Corporal Kreutz advised that two police officers and one other witness in the area of the base were now observing the objects, which were a pulsating, brilliant white and moving in a jerky fashion at cloud height. A report was going to be sent to National Defence Headquarters in Ottawa. The log entry ends here as far as the UFO report is concerned.

One thing that is not clear from all the accounts is whether the objects were in view at the same time as the jets. The jets searched the area up to 30,000 feet, yet the objects were last reported at 72,000 feet. While the jets' radar can extend beyond the altitude capability of the airplane, there is no indication of the range actually used. That nothing was reported by the jets is not an indication that no physical objects were present. The reports were consistent among all ground observers, and the simultaneous visual and radar corroboration of the rapid ascent of the object would tend to rule out planets, stars, and temperature inversion effects. The only certainty is that something highly unusual occurred over the Sudbury skies that morning.

It is clear from the foregoing that the Department of National Defence was still very much in the UFO picture, depending on the nature of the sighting, even though the National Research Council was now the official custodian of reports. In fact, the

Director of Operations was still going to receive reports, under CFAO 71-6. This order remained in effect until 1988 before being removed from the books. On September 27, 1988, a letter of clarification was sent out across the department. It stated that deletion of the CFAO order meant only that the National Defence Operations Centre (NDOC) was no longer interested in receiving UFO reports. All other addressees, however, including Air Command Operations Centre, Winnipeg, NORAD Cheyenne Mtn. Complex CO/J3Y, and Fighter Group Headquarters FGHQ North Bay/SSO Int., were still interested in getting those reports. Hence, apart from the NRC and early DND files, numerous other records must yet exist.

Most of the UFO files held at the National Archives in Ottawa are now open. Generally, they house the National Research Council records. In 1993 the archives declassified more files that had been turned over by the NRC. These files detail numerous reported sightings. For example, in June 1992 over a dozen people in Winnipeg spotted a circular object, which was also photographed.

In another incident, in Taber, Alberta, on July 6, 1992, at 3:23 a.m., a fifteen-year-old watching television heard a car or truck starting up. Looking out, she saw red, white, yellow, and blue lights flashing on and off. Moving to a better vantage point at the kitchen window, she saw a huge, dull gray or black object hovering 20 or 30 meters (60 to 100 feet) away at tree top–level. She watched for a few minutes, after which she became scared and ran to hide under her bed covers. She felt at that point that she had blacked out. Upon investigation, the RCMP found small, fresh impressions in the ground, three inches deep, four inches across, and some in a straight line three feet apart. They led to the area under which the object had hovered.

On December 28, 1992, a United Airlines 737 flying west

reported an object at 39,000 feet, moving east at 460 knots. Sparks were seen emanating from the back. Air traffic control in Edmonton, Alberta, reported no radar track or other aircraft in the vicinity.

On August 2, 1993, in Mission, British Columbia, a mother, her fourteen-year-old daughter, and a friend of her daughter reported a dark, triangular-shaped object with reddish brown lights. It was 11:30 p.m. No sound was heard.

In 1992 an impressive videotape was sent anonymously to UFO researcher and former NASA mission specialist Bob Oechsler. Aired on the television program *Unsolved Mysteries*, the video showed the apparent landing of a mysterious object with a flashing beacon at its top.

The incident had actually taken place near Carp, Ontario, west of Ottawa, in August 1991. With the video were six pages of documents purporting to be from DND, along with a map of the area and a photograph of what appears to be an alien being. The videotape itself was signed "Guardian" and included a thumbprint but no other identifiers.

Oechsler believes that the documents were in fact forgeries. The video, however, is another matter. A specialist in analyzing photographs, Oechsler believes that the video depicts a large, solid object of unknown origin and that the entire event is real, not a hoax.

The UFO was reported by resident Dianne Lambenek. Oechsler visited her in May 1992. What she explained she saw in the distance exactly matched the images on the videotape. A search of the landing site showed a 50-foot-diameter area in which all plant life was dead. The plants were wilted, a description also common to some of the sightings mentioned above. Plant samples showed a high titanium content.

Captain Louis Nadeau, the base information officer at Canadian

Forces Base Uplands in Ottawa, confirmed that something was seen on the night in question. Unmarked helicopters were also reported seen in the area. The helicopters have been described as all black with double rotors. They came within 10 feet of the Lambenek household. Nadeau has stated that these were not DND helicopters and were likely not even Canadian but that due to the nature of their flight path, they would have remained undetected and unmonitored.

Other witnesses to the event have since come forward, including one who passed a lie detector test and claimed she boarded the craft. Additional sightings have also occurred in the area. One group of researchers claims that the entire incident was in fact a hoax perpetrated by an acquaintance of Lambenek, but Oechsler maintains that this was not the case. He has continued his own investigations and is preparing a book on the subject.

And sightings continue. One of the more interesting of the recent sightings occurred on the evening of January 6, 1995, as a British Airways 737 approached Manchester Airport in northern England. The tower had just given clearance for the aircraft to descend to 4,000 feet when the following conversation between the pilot of the BA 737 and the tower was recorded:

BA 737: We just had something go down the RHS [right-hand side] just above us very fast.
Tower: Well there's nothing seen on radar. Was it an ac [aircraft]?
BA 737: Well, it had lights, it went down the starboard side very quick.
Tower: And above you?
BA 737: Er, just slightly above us, yeah.
Tower: Keep an eye out for something, er, I can't see anything at all at the moment so, er, must have, er,

been very fast or gone down very quickly after it passed you think.

BA 737: OK. Well, there you go![3]

Subsequent investigation by the Civil Aviation Authority (CAA) revealed that the pilot viewed the object for about two seconds as it crossed the right-hand windscreen and side window of the aircraft. He described it as wedge-shaped with a number of small white lights, similar to a Christmas tree. He did not know how far away the object was but felt that it was very close.

The 737's first officer also saw the object pass by the right side of the aircraft at high speed. He described it as a dark, wedge-shaped object with what might have been a black stripe down the side. He drew a diagram of the object which matched that which the pilot had independently drawn. His description differed from the pilot's only with reference to the tiny lights. The first officer thought that perhaps the object was illuminated by the 737's own landing lights, which were switched on at the time. He estimated that the object was somewhere between the size of a light aircraft and a jet stream. He was uncertain how far away it was but said he instinctively "ducked" as it flew by.

Could it have been a Stealth aircraft? Given its wedge shape and dark appearance, the Stealth immediately comes to mind. But the first officer had seen Stealth planes before and claims he would have recognized the object as such. In spite of the first officer's knowledge of the Stealth, the investigating group from the CAA checked with military authorities on the possibility of a Stealth aircraft in the vicinity. They found "no evidence of this from any official source." Official denial, plus the improbability that military activity would take place so close to a busy airport with or without notifying the CAA, more or less ruled out any possibility that the UFO was in fact a Stealth. A check was also made to determine if the object might have been a hang glider, paraglider, or ultralight aircraft. Again the answer was negative.

Although the Boeing was tracked on the ground radar at the time, the object was not. The investigators did not find this unusual because the radar had weather suppressors which may have been turned on at the time. In that case, *if* the object gave a poor radar response, the radar would interpret it as weather phenomena and not show it. The CAA investigating group finally listed the incident as unresolved but made the following comment:

. . . this report, submitted by two responsible airline pilots, was considered seriously and we wish to commend the pilots for their courage in submitting it, and their company, whose enlightened attitude made it possible. Reports such as these are often the object of derision, but the Group hopes that this example will encourage pilots who experience unusual sightings to report them without fear of ridicule.[4]

Ten

Operation Perception Management

"But through official secrecy and ridicule, many citizens are led to believe the unknown flying objects are nonsense."[1]

Vice Admiral R. H. Hillenkoetter (retired), former director of the CIA, February 28, 1960

Is there a cover-up of real close encounters — encounters with extraterrestrial spacecraft and perhaps their occupants? Or are the countless reports a series of hoaxes committed over the space of more than a century? Are they optical illusions? Secret weapons? Natural phenomena? Take your pick. But remember, none of the above is necessarily *the* explanation. There may well be some of each, a mixed bag of explanations which leaves us with a burning desire to know the truth because inside, most of us want to believe we are not alone in this vast universe. Many are hopeful that there are beings more intelligent than we, with an even more advanced technology, who will appear and supply us with answers to life's mysteries.

When one enters the realm of UFOs, one truly does enter a twilight zone, a place where fact and fiction are intertwined and conventional wisdom suffers a resounding defeat. Many of those who have made a career out of the study of UFOs have been disappointed in their search for the ever-elusive truth. As Dr. Hynek said in reflecting on his own involvement, "The witnesses I interviewed *could* have been lying, *could* have been insane, or *could* have been hallucinating collectively — but I do not think so."[2]

Corroboration by photographic and radar evidence notwithstanding, the nature of what was actually seen by eyewitnesses comes down to a judgment call, since the evidence itself is never very specific.

Added to this are the secrecy and deliberate campaign of disinformation which have been imposed over a long period of time, dogging researchers and investigators in search of the truth. Disinformation is the fabrication of stories and evidence for the purposes of misleading or discrediting witnesses and researchers alike. Disinformation creates a smoke screen behind which to hide the truth. *Jane's Defense Weekly* has reported that the USAF is officially authorized to orchestrate disinformation campaigns. Is it possible that these campaigns have reached into Canada? Is this what happened to Wilbert Smith?

The Smith case contains some interesting parallels to another UFO case involving an American, Dr. Paul Bennewitz. A physicist, Bennewitz ran a small firm in Albuquerque, New Mexico. From his home he recorded on film numerous incidents of strange lights flying in from the direction of Kirtland Air Force Base in Albuquerque, over the Manzano Nuclear Weapons Storage Facility and south towards the Coyote Canyon test area. He also recorded a low-frequency beep which would accompany the objects. He believed the beeps were signals of some sort. He called his investigative effort Project Beta.

In 1979, through a friend, psychologist Dr. Leo Sprinkle, Bennewitz became involved in the hypnotic regression session of a woman who claimed she had been abducted by aliens. Under hypnosis the woman revealed that the aliens were involved in cattle mutilations, taking the pieces for their own experimentation. She also spoke of implant devices, which Bennewitz theorized were for some kind of control.

He published these findings and later became convinced that the aliens had struck a deal with the U.S. government allowing them to continue their experiments, in exchange for technology. Now, however, the aliens were effecting a double cross and he needed to somehow expose them. Bennewitz's theories and claims made their way into mainstream UFO literature to the point where many now believe the story of the "malevolent gray aliens" to be true. As well, claims of implants in human abductees have risen sharply since the Bennewitz revelations.

Did the CIA figure in the Bennewitz story? William Moore, a UFO researcher and co-author of *The Roswell Incident*, discovered through contacts at the Air Force Office of Special Investigations (AFOSI) that a disinformation campaign against Bennewitz had been ongoing since 1980. Counterintelligence agents from several agencies told Bennewitz of the broken treaties with the aliens, of implants and technology exchanges gone sour, of a group of benevolent aliens, the "whites," and so on. Laden with promises that he would receive classified information about the UFOs, Moore ended up being a participant for four years, to help determine the effectiveness of the disinformation campaign against Bennewitz. Moore was apparently even given official yet doctored documents to pass on to the unsuspecting physicist.

Moore claims he never discovered why Bennewitz had been targeted. Whether it was because he was uncovering information he was not supposed to uncover, about either UFOs or secret government projects, or whether he was an unwitting participant in a larger exercise in psychological warfare, is unclear. For his part, Bennewitz became obsessed, believing that the aliens were feeding him chemicals. Unable to sleep, he eventually suffered a breakdown.

Eventually Moore himself would receive the now infamous Majestic Twelve or MJ-12 documents. These documents, stamped "TOP SECRET/EYES ONLY," purport that flying saucers did crash and were recovered, along with alien bodies. They give the first crash as occurring at Roswell, New Mexico, in 1947. They state that a second crash occurred in Texas in December 1950, near the Mexican border. According to the MJ-12 documents, the man in charge of the group of twelve individuals selected to analyze the material and bodies was Dr. Vannevar Bush. Unfortunately, while there may be elements of truth in the documents, as Stanton Friedman has vigorously and meticulously pointed out, they are still being declared a hoax by skeptics. The disinformation campaign proved to be most effective.

Recognizing the reality of such disinformation campaigns allows us to look at Wilbert Smith's beliefs and actions in a different light. Smith was told about the alien bodies and the crashed disks by Dr. Sarbacher. He also found out that a small group under Bush was involved in the analysis. This information could very well have been legitimate. Smith was a well-known and respected engineer interested in magnetic propulsion, and his help may initially have been sought in uncovering the propulsive secrets of the crashed disk. He was also being encouraged in this endeavor by Dr. Omond Solandt, Bush's friend and confidant. But Smith may have run afoul of the confidence he had established when he violated Solandt's request not to speak to the media but to keep matters confidential.

Smith went public on several fronts. He made public statements regarding the reality of the UFOs as extraterrestrial alien vehicles, and he disclosed the existence of his research station in Shirley's Bay. In 1959, at an engineering conference in Ottawa, he also made statements that pieces of crashed disks existed but were held under tight security.

Someone may have decided that it would not be long before Smith would reveal Sarbacher as the source of his original information. If Smith were given false information in the guise of it being true, he might discredit himself, as Bennewitz did, by going public with it.

A case in point concerns a piece of metal allegedly shot off a UFO by a USAF fighter. The incident occurred in July 1952 over Washington, D.C. During one night's wave of sightings, a military jet was scrambled to chase after the objects. The pilot was able to lock on with his radar and fire a round of shots. A glowing fragment was seen to break off the UFO and was later retrieved by ground personnel. It was this fragment, or a piece of it, that was eventually turned over to Smith for analysis. After completing his examination of the fragment, Smith returned it to a group much higher than the air force or the Central Intelligence Agency. This must have been the analysis group headed by Bush.

Smith confirmed this story to a couple of researchers in November 1961, but he did not reveal how he came into possession of the fragment other than say that it was sent to him. He also never revealed the identity of those to whom he returned the fragment. There is no indication that he ever discussed the matter with anyone associated with Project Magnet or Project

Second Storey, but according to Arthur Bray, Smith's wife had seen the fragment.

The incident is also discussed in the book titled *Scientific Study of Unidentified Flying Objects* published in 1969. This was a two-year study on UFOs conducted under the direction of Dr. Edward Condon of the University of Colorado, shortly after the demise of Blue Book and on behalf of the United States Air Force. Known as the Condon Committee, this was the same group that had reviewed the Michalak case through Dr. Craig. The Condon report, as the study has become known, has been regarded as part of a cover-up, due to leaked information suggesting that Condon was bent on dismissing the whole UFO phenomenon even before the study was officially begun. In fact, this was the general conclusion of the study in spite of the fact that it cited numerous cases where the researchers concluded there was no earthly explanation for what was seen and in some instances photographed.

In the case of the alleged Smith fragment, however, the Condon Committee undertook a detailed review. The committee confirmed that Project Blue Book had no information relating to the occurrence. More importantly, there was no Lieutenant Commander Frank Thompson of the U.S. Navy, an official who had supposedly confirmed the incident and the existence of the fragment. Moreover, none of the UFO reports that night made any references to any shots being fired, and it was deemed foolish that shots would ever be fired over the city unnecessarily. The implication was, of course, that the shooting incident had never happened. Where then did Smith's fragment come from?

One answer may be contained in the same Condon report. It notes that in 1953 the CIA was "party to a scheme to 'debunk' the UFOs."[3] Perhaps Smith, like Bennewitz, was the victim of a CIA disinformation campaign. Had he gotten too close as a result of Sarbacher's information? Over the years, Smith would receive numerous pieces of flying saucers for analysis, but were any of them genuine and would anyone take his analysis seriously?

Another aspect of possible government action to discredit Smith involves his role in the CIA's telepathic experiments with regard to UFOs. The CIA claimed to have a woman who was in contact with an alien being (shades of Bennewitz). She would write out the alien's messages. As previously recounted, Smith kept in touch with the woman and thereby maintained contact with the alien, whose name was AFFA.

Was the woman a genuine psychic, or at least someone who believed she was, or was she an agent of the CIA? And again, would anyone have seriously believed Smith, a man involved with psychics? Smith was a man who really wanted to believe, and because he wanted to believe, he may have given in uncritically to the "willing suspension of disbelief." Smith used the information from the alien (via the psychic) to write his work *The New Science*. But was it new science or just bad science? Had the entire episode been set up by the CIA? After all, it occurred at a time when the CIA and the Canadian Defence Research Board were collaborating on covert psychological experiments, research which, when revealed, would become infamous as one of the most blatant civil and human rights violations of modern times.

In the 1980s it was revealed that the CIA had conducted LSD mind-control experiments on unwitting patients in Canada. Once proven, the revelations made headlines. The CIA's not-so-brief foray into mind-control experiments actually began in 1950, under Project Bluebird. In 1951 the CIA co-ordinated efforts with the U.S. military under Project Artichoke and in 1953 it became Project MKULTRA. Part of the MKULTRA mandate was:

> . . . implanting suggestions and other forms of mental control . . . designed to investigate methods to influence

memory, thought, attitude, motivation, and ultimately human behaviour.[4]

The CIA repeatedly denied the claims but it has since been established that the experiments were carried out on patients at the Allan Memorial Institute of Psychiatry in Montreal. Patients suffered from the effects of the drugs and the experiments for years afterward, and it is said that at least one death could be attributed to this affair. Suits brought against the American government were successful and many shocking details were revealed during the court cases. The point here is that what was being planted in people's minds was not being planted by aliens. The use of hallucinogenic drugs and other experiments on the human mind were added to disinformation as weapons with which to discredit those who might otherwise have appeared credible. It does not seem far-fetched that Wilbert Smith, the willing believer, was part of a larger experiment.

According to John Robert Colombo, the CIA was concerned that the Soviets and Chinese were also conducting mind-control experiments. The CIA initiated its own program, MKULTRA, so as not to be left behind. Canada became involved on June 1, 1951, at a secret meeting at the Ritz-Carlton Hotel in Montreal. Two CIA representatives were present, as well as Sir Henry Tizard of the British Defence Research Board. The other individual present was Dr. Solandt of the Canadian Defence Research Board.

The Defence Research Board had already been financing the isolation research of Canadian psychiatrist Dr. O. Hebb. MKULTRA would become an extension of that work, under Dr. Ewen Cameron of the Allan Memorial Institute. Solandt was connected to both MKULTRA and Wilbert Smith. When Smith violated Solandt's confidence by going to the media, Smith may have become an unwitting participant in MKULTRA. While this is speculation, the possibility cannot be ignored.

Smith had been influenced in his work by Donald Keyhoe's writings and had in turn written articles for him. Keyhoe was continually after the USAF to admit to the reality of UFOs as extraterrestrial craft. He continually challenged the air force and stated that a massive cover-up was underway. He eventually became the director of the National Investigations Committee on Aerial Phenomena, or NICAP for short. NICAP was most bothersome to the USAF and was also an irritant to Canadian officials. A memo written for the Canadian Chief of the Air Staff in 1963, in response to a query from a private citizen, states that the individual writing:

> . . . is a member of an organization known as the "National Committee on Aerial Phenomena" (NICAP) . . . This organization is dedicated to the beliefs that "flying saucers" (in the more exotic sense) exist, that this fact is being concealed from the public by the U.S.A.F. and the RCAF, and that its members are serving the public interest by attempting to expose this official censorship . . . The proposed reply . . . is quite lengthy and informative (though not specific) in the hope that it may discourage further inquiries from this particular source.[5]

By 1957 Wilbert Smith had become NICAP's Canadian chairman. Through him, the whole NICAP organization, and Keyhoe in particular, could be targeted for disinformation.

According to author Timothy Good, the CIA developed an interest in NICAP, which had a solid investigative team. Since NICAP had been approached by the KGB, the CIA could use the committee to monitor this agency. NICAP had kept the subject of UFOs alive, despite government attempts to debunk it. NICAP's large following put the organization in a position to influence mass thinking. Interestingly, when Keyhoe was removed as NICAP's director in 1969, the man responsible was Chairman of the Board Colonel Joseph Bryan III, former chief of the CIA's psychological warfare staff. That Smith had become a target for disinformation, perhaps after learning too much and going public, is not necessarily an implausible stretch in logic, given what was going on with MKULTRA, Solandt, NICAP, and the CIA. No doubt there exist other targets for disinformation as well.

Over the years, reports have surfaced that films exist of military personnel making contact with aliens. At least one incident was filmed and purportedly shows a craft hovering and then landing. A panel slides open and three "men" in jumpsuits come out and converse with military personnel and scientists before moving to an office location. Other reports have stated that films exist of the Roswell recovery, and in 1995 the alien autopsy film was shown on television.

Are these films, or in some cases their alleged existence, part of a disinformation campaign or some kind of large-scale psychological warfare experiment? This author received information that such films were supposedly shown to select military personnel and attachés with the expectation that they would believe the craft came from outer space. The apparent object of showing such films was the hope that the information gleaned from them would then be leaked out. The ultimate target of this disinformation was the Soviets. Presumably it was believed that the Soviets could be tricked into thinking the U.S. had made contact with aliens and were now in possession of superior technology; all part of cold war strategy.

Fantasy? Again according to Timothy Good, Miles Copeland, a CIA intelligence officer, advised him of a plan to spread UFO stories in China. It happened in the early sixties. Several fictional accounts were reported in various areas. The objective was to "keep the Chinese off balance . . ."⁶ But, Good adds, some of the stories were picked up by cult groups in the United States. Like in the case of MKULTRA, the intent was to shape beliefs and perhaps effect behavior in other countries. According to the information received by this author, the name of the operation was Perception Management. Is Perception Management real, or just another piece of disinformation?

The concept of perception management is a valid one in intelligence circles and a distinction is made between it and straight disinformation. The latter is used to mislead an opponent or discredit him or her by supplying false information. Perception management on the other hand "is the attempt to lead an enemy to certain conclusions by carefully fashioning what he [or she] perceives." For example, when large-scale troop movements are suddenly reported in one country, analysts in the target country begin speculating as to their significance, and sometimes unnecessary actions and countermeasures are taken.

In the case of the UFO films of contact with aliens, the target country would hear of their reality through the normal espionage channels and react accordingly. In addition to influencing behavior, a secondary effect would be to confuse and discredit the entire subject with the ultimate revelation of the hoax.

Solandt, MKULTRA, Smith, and Project Y were all interconnected. It has been suggested that Project Y was a smoke screen, perhaps part of perception management, to help hide the true facts behind the flying saucers, much like the balloon cover story was used to obscure the Roswell incident when it first surfaced.

On September 18, 1994, the *Ottawa Citizen* and other newspapers ran the following headline: "Air Force report shoots down UFO theories about 1947 crash."⁷ The crash being referred to was, naturally, the Roswell incident. Congressman Steven H. Schiff of New Mexico inquired about records concerning the crash and was stonewalled by the USAF. In February 1994 he was successful in getting the General Accounting Office (GAO) to initiate an audit to locate all records related to the crash. The results of this audit would eventually show that some records from Roswell had indeed been destroyed, but who destroyed them, by what authority, and what they contained haven't been determined.

In anticipation of the GAO investigation, the air force undertook to locate all the records it could. Witnesses who might have had a recollection of the incident were interviewed, and a blanket clearance was given to those who might otherwise have believed they were still under oath, in order to allow them to come forward.

Writing in *Watch the Skies*, author Curtis Peebles recalls the Roswell case. He notes that the debris had been identified as a Rawin Target and a weather balloon, the Rawin Target being the radar reflector. This became the official explanation and the incident is cited as explained, with no alien saucers of which to speak. Researchers, however, showed that no weather balloons were launched at the time of the crash and point to the fact that Major Jesse Marcel, who examined some of the wreckage and who was familiar with weather balloons, did not recognize it as such.

The *Ottawa Citizen* article mentioned above notes an interesting admission: "At the time, the Air Force said the wreckage was that of a weather balloon, *a white lie* [italics mine] . . ."[8] In their 1994 report, the USAF admitted that the debris was not from a weather balloon, implying that the weather balloon story was disinformation, concocted to effectively kill the story and any further inquiries about it.

In the face of the GAO investigation, the USAF report still maintained that a balloon was involved but claimed that it was from a top-secret affair called Project Mogul. The purpose of Mogul was to send aloft sensing devices that could detect nuclear explosions in the Soviet Union. In this way the United States could monitor Soviet atomic activities. The report noted that the reason the debris was misidentified as a weather balloon was probably that the balloons and materials involved were similar. This, despite the fact that a "black box" supposedly containing Mogul instruments was also found. It seems odd that such secrecy would be placed on Project Mogul and that only the fear of a government investigation begun in 1994 would finally force the facts out into the open. After all, Mogul did not represent a leap in technology which had to be kept secret at all costs.

Marcel did not recognize the debris as coming from any balloon device. Was Mogul balloon material that difficult to recognize? In 1956 a burst balloon and radiosonde equipment was found in New Brunswick. It was immediately identified as such and returned to the U.S. military without any mystery. Yet with Roswell, an experienced officer failed to recognize the device. As well, people have come forward with tales of seeing spacecraft, alien bodies, anything but balloons.

In addition to the Mogul explanation, the USAF report indicated that a study of alien technology and recovered craft would come under the category of Special Access Programs or SAPs and that there was no SAP related to extraterrestrial spacecraft and aliens. Yet *Jane's Defense Weekly* pointed out in 1992 that there is a subcategory of SAPs called "waived programs" which do not have to be disclosed in the same manner. Could the Roswell incident have fallen under the category of waived programs? Indeed, why should it fall under any such category at all, and would it necessarily remain under the purview of the USAF? *Jane's*, noting that the Department of Defense authorizes the spread of misleading information, made the following comment: "Once we know that the DOD practices this kind of deception, it becomes harder to discern what is real and what is not."[9]

Is the U.S. military spreading disinformation about Roswell? There are those who would contend that the answer is yes, based on the stories told by witnesses coming forward. The report itself acknowledges that some will scream cover-up when they read about the Project Mogul explanation. As for the multitude of witnesses coming forward, they are dismissed in the report as having, "in the 'fog of time,' misinterpreted past events."[10]

If one could recall with clarity where he or she was at the time of President Kennedy's assassination, for example, it seems reasonable that one could also recall any involvement with extraterrestrial spacecraft and aliens. Such an event is simply too extraordinary to forget or grossly misinterpret.

Given all the circumstances, it seems that in 1950 Wilbert Smith was originally told the truth about flying saucers. There was as yet no covert reason to give him false information or even to meet with him. Smith may *later* have become a victim of a disinformation campaign when he began going public, in much the same way that Paul Bennewitz became a target. Project Y was probably part of the smoke screen but may also have contributed to a black program of building a flying saucer, and the Roswell incident, which gave rise to the renewed interest in crashed disks, is still being hushed up by the USAF.

Eleven

The Challenge

"The truth is out there."

The X-Files, television program

Countless witnesses have stated that they were threatened by military personnel after the Roswell story broke in 1947. Were their memories really clouded by the "fog of time," or was this explanation just another excuse by the military?

Perhaps the Roswell citizens were perpetrators of one of the greatest pranks in modern history. Yet if any of these people were witness to a murder, their testimony might send a criminal to execution, and would be taken seriously. On the subject of UFO wreckage and alien bodies, however, they are not to be believed. Short of using lie detector tests, checking the credibility of these witnesses remains a difficult task (not that lie detector tests are

100 percent reliable either). But the credibility of the military and government establishments is also very much in question. How can *their* credibility be measured?

Who told the world that U-2 spy plane overflights were actually gathering meteorological data and nothing more? Who orchestrated the utilization of LSD for psychological experiments on unsuspecting citizens in the United States and Canada? Who toyed with Paul Bennewitz's mind and quite possibly Wilbert Smith's mind as well? Who kept the identity of the Stealth Fighter hidden while it flew for over ten years? Who admitted to having performed over 800 radiation tests, including the willful injection of plutonium, on unsuspecting human subjects, in the forties? Government, in its many guises and under the auspices of its many departments, has been responsible for too many questionable actions to walk away with its credibility untarnished. At best, cold war mentality and secret military programs affected the judgment of those in power; at worst, there were lies, cover-ups, and definite violations of human and civil rights. Indeed, there seems to have been something of both.

In the minds of many, secrecy was justified by the cold war, and the choice of means to secure secrecy illustrated a blatant example of the end justifying the means. According to John Morton Blum, Woodward Professor of History at Yale University:

> . . . they [Dr. Vannevar Bush and Dr. James B. Conant, as well as their immediate associates] became increasingly involved in the prototypical defense establishment of the war years, the unofficial company, brought together by common interests in a common cause, of senior men from the War Department, the armed services, the war industries, and the scientific community. It was therefore easy for Bush and Conant to conclude, when in 1943 the British requested

a free exchange of information, that secret data, like the construction and operation of facilities for its use, should remain accessible exclusively to Americans . . .[1]

This American attitude anticipated postwar policy, and in the face of the cold war and the Korean War, the means of achieving secrecy went beyond toleration and credibility was lost. But on it went. Clearly, millions were spent on gathering information while denials of the existence of UFOs continued.

Who has the greater credibility, the citizens of Roswell or the various government agencies that have provided "explanations"? Actually, the real question is, why did the military and the government behave the way they did, if (for example) the Roswell disk was just a balloon?

Two months after the incident at Roswell, General Nathan Twining admitted in a secret memo that the UFO phenomenon was something real. But why was the memo kept secret if it was known that the UFO reports were nonsense? Three months after the Twining memo, Project Sign was established. It was close to reaching the conclusion that the saucers were interplanetary vehicles when it was terminated and renamed Project Grudge. Project Grudge, to no one's surprise, ended up debunking all UFO reports.

Why, if the Grudge conclusions were accurate, did the Canadian Minister of National Defence order the Department of National Defence, through Dr. Solandt and the Defence Research Board, to study and analyze flying saucer reports in 1950? Did the Minister know something the rest of us did not? Was he influenced by Vannevar Bush when the two, along with Solandt, met in 1948? Shortly after the Minister's request to Solandt, Wilbert Smith was put in touch with Dr. Sarbacher, through the Canadian Embassy and Lieutenant Commander (Navy) James

Stewart Bremner. Sarbacher ended up telling Smith that the stories of crashed saucers and alien bodies were all true and that Smith's knowledge in geomagnetics might assist the team under Vannevar Bush in solving the propulsion problem. Coincidence?

Bush's commitment to secrecy and his government's means to achieve it did allow the British and the Canadians to know some details on a "need to know" basis.

How did James Stewart Bremner find Sarbacher, and why did he bother? Did he find out through Rear Admiral J. Tate, the man who in 1951 told him that the prototype of a nuclear-powered aircraft was about to be completed? Why did Bremner not simply dismiss Smith as a crackpot and discard the whole UFO mess if, as the Grudge report concluded, all the sightings were hysteria? Not only did this not happen but Solandt, who initially encouraged Smith, began to distance himself from Smith once the latter started going public with his information. Furthermore, why was the Central Intelligence Agency monitoring worldwide reports of UFOs and sending copies to DND if all the sightings were figments of people's imaginations? Why was Blue Book's Special Report No. 14 initially hidden?

The UFO question remained open after the Grudge report was submitted, and Project Blue Book was begun to continue the studies. In Canada, in addition to Smith's work, Project Second Storey was initiated. With both Blue Book and Second Storey there is evidence that the best reports were not submitted, in spite of the fact that both projects were headed by hardnosed, skeptical astronomers bent on dismissing the subject: Millman in Canada and Hynek in the U.S. Was this the beginning of a cover-up, or an opportunity, at least in Canada, to discredit Smith and others?

After Millman and Solandt failed to endorse any of Smith's assertions about the extraterrestrial nature of the saucers, he was left to continue his work on his own. Both his own Department of Transport and DND issued denials that Smith had ever been officially supported in his UFO work, yet Project Magnet was made official by both departments. There are even letters on file, sent in response to inquiries from the public, which suggest that Smith had become the Canadian NICAP chairman, against the advice from his department. Why all the negativism towards Smith? Even if his department felt Smith had become an embarrassment, there was no need to deny the support he was given. After all, he remained highly regarded as an engineer and in 1957 was appointed Superintendent of Radio Regulations Engineering for Canada.

Sarbacher insisted in 1986 that as far as he was concerned, everything he had revealed to Smith was true. The question might then be asked if Sarbacher hadn't been lied to by his own colleagues. This seems unlikely, as he was asked several times to join the investigation team but was unable to do so. Why continue the joke for so long, and why complicate it by adding that telepathic communication was part of the investigation?

When Smith became involved with the CIA, did he also become the victim of a disinformation campaign — as did Paul Bennewitz years later? Why else would the CIA concoct such a story for Smith? And why was Smith sent phony pieces of metal to analyze?

Was the Avrocar, or Silver Bug as it was known in secret military circles, part of a disinformation campaign, or a way to obtain needed technical data for what has been dubbed Project Ladybug? Did Stefan Michalak encounter one of these in 1967, at a time when other reports have indicated that such craft existed?

Later in the fifties, the Americans produced the CIRVIS/MERINT/JANAP 146 procedures for reporting UFOs. The United States Air Force produced its own guidelines, Air Force Regulation 200-202, and in Canada, Canadian Forces

Administrative Order 71-6 was developed for UFO reporting. Interestingly, CIRVIS/MERINT gave a very clear definition of UFOs as flying saucers and not just some unidentifiable thing in the sky. Why all the fuss and effort over a supposed silly subject?

Then there is the secrecy surrounding the infamous Area 51 in the New Mexico desert. For years, the USAF denied the existence of this closely guarded area, even though buildings could be seen in the distance. The perimeter fence around this nonexistent area warns would-be curiosity seekers that lethal force will be used against trespassers. This is not in itself uncommon around secret military installations, but there is more.

It has been said that the area is used for testing secret aircraft like the Stealth fighter/bomber and SR-71 Blackbird, and this is true enough in the sector known as the Tonopah range. But what is going on in Dreamland over Groom Lake? UFOs have been reported over this area, and in the eighties, Bob Lazar, an individual claiming to be a former employee at Area 51, claimed the U.S. government was test-flying and studying extraterrestrial flying saucers there.

During the Gulf War, Captain Wolf Hassenklover (Canada) was involved in a military exercise at Nellis Air Force Base in which radar equipment aboard a Hercules aircraft was being tested. The exercise took place over the desert and near Area 51. The exercise was scheduled to continue for eleven days but was abruptly terminated several days early. Through crew error, the aircraft skirted one edge of Area 51, just south of Bald Mountain. On its return to Nellis Air Force Base, the military police were waiting. The aircraft was examined for cameras and film, and the exercise was ended. What surprised the Canadians was that during their debriefing, they were shown videotape of their plane crossing the perimeter. They had not expected such a high degree of monitoring.

Because the authorities knew exactly what had happened and because it was a Canadian plane, the crew were simply sent packing. They were told, however, that had this happened to an American pilot, mistake or not, the punishment would have been far more severe.

Again, this behavior is understandable if secret research was in fact being conducted. What does not make sense is the rest of what the crew were told. It seems that if an aircraft is in trouble, it will, reluctantly, be allowed to land at the Tonopah range. No one should even think, however, about making an emergency landing in Dreamland. The crew were told that such a landing would never be allowed to occur in one piece. If this is true, what secret could be so deadly that it must be protected at all cost?

The evidence, although circumstantial, seems to show that not only are UFOs from another world being harbored there, but there is and has been an ongoing cover-up and a campaign of officially sanctioned disinformation and deception.

The UFO phenomenon is one of the most intriguing and scientifically challenging mysteries facing us. Sightings have occurred throughout recorded history and reports continue to criss-cross continents today. Science, which requires something tangible to measure, in fact has not been able to explain what is going on, possibly because science has been denied the real evidence. This prospect makes the challenge of learning the truth even more difficult. It is rather like disputing the existence of God; the arguments always boil down to a question of belief.

If governments truly know something, as suggested by their actions, why all the secrecy? It has been suggested that revealing the existence of extraterrestrial beings would create widespread panic. Some authors point to the *War of the Worlds* broadcast in the thirties and the panic it caused. There are obvious differences, however. Orson Welles presented the fictional H. G. Wells story, an attack on Earth by Martians — Martians who systematically destroyed everything in their path. As well, his audience had not been exposed to science in the way this generation has been exposed. Nor had the computer revolution taken place. Man had not yet walked on the moon and the magic of such films as *Star Trek* and *ET* was yet to be produced.

Others have suggested that military secrets of alien technology would require protection from enemy countries. Possibly the technology would be used to build superior military weaponry and would therefore need to be protected. On the other hand, the government and the military themselves might be questioned by the citizens they serve, if it was revealed that aliens were regularly violating our airspace and we could do nothing about it. Some others also contend that nations would collapse and economies would be in ruins.

And of course, there is plain old capitalist competition. As Dr. Blum notes:

> Though neither Great Britain or Canada intended to manufacture fissionable materials during the war, both wanted American information in order to use it for postwar construction of new sources of energy. With characteristic Yankee doubts about English [and by extension Canadian] motives, doubts that most Americans probably would have harbored had they known about the issue, Bush and Conant suspected that the British were interested primarily in postwar commercial enterprises . . .[2]

This attitude of protectionism is still very much in evidence.

The likelihood, then, that the U.S. government will reveal all appears slim at best. Suppose for a moment, however, that it is indeed true. Numerous citizens who have seen or investigated

UFOs have claimed over the years that they were followed, had their phones tapped, or otherwise had their rights abused in some way. People like Glenn Dennis, the mortician in the Roswell episode, claim to have been physically threatened. Others claim their families were also threatened should they ever attempt to reveal all. That some of these claims should be taken seriously is evidenced by the comments in *Aviation Week & Space Technology* magazine, that people working on black programs, for example, have had their civil rights abused and that the code of silence rivals that of the Mafia. An admission by the government, then, about the reality of UFOs as extraterrestrial in origin would lend credibility to these statements of threats and coercion made by witnesses who have come forward. This could open a Pandora's box of ensuing litigation. Perhaps this is one reason for all the secrecy.

While a few people may find some of this to be old news, the vast majority of citizens still believe that governments would never go to such lengths. They believe that while there may be some corruption, by and large that is the extent of it, that cover-ups do not exist. They forget that it took considerable effort to finally prove, and force the government to admit to, its LSD and radiation experiments. And those who came forward then were not initially believed either.

Jim Bronskill of Southam News has recently reported that "Canada's 'X-Files' Soon May Become Ex-files . . ."[3] It seems that Canada's National Research Council is cutting the department that for many years collected the reports of sightings of UFOs from various Canadian agencies and from the general public. It is hoped that reports will continue to be placed in the National Archives and that one of the UFO monitoring organizations will take over the investigation of such reports. Unprobed tales of sightings can only increase speculation, but the worst possible decision would be to send the most interesting and reputable reports into the secret vaults of the military or the North American Air Defense Command. The cries of "cover-up!" will continue as long as anything less than full disclosure exists.

The bottom line is that one cannot and must not tread naively into this quagmire of fact and fiction. One must remain objective and open-minded on all fronts, no matter how bizarre or fantastic the hypothesis, until hard corroborating evidence can be obtained. Above all, one must not become paranoid but be willing to accept the truth, no matter how extraordinary it might be. It is out there, and someday it will be revealed.

Postscript

In 1997, shortly after the publication of the hardcover edition of this book, the USAF released its final report on the Roswell incident. Entitled "The Roswell Report: Case Closed," the report reiterates the theory that it was a balloon that was recovered in 1947 at the Roswell crash site, not a UFO. In the report, the USAF claims that the bodies witnesses saw were actually military crash-test dummies, used in the testing of military hardware. The report also claims that the ambulances in Roswell were on hand to respond to military aircraft crashes. Because the use of crash-test dummies and the aircraft crashes occurred separately and well after the 1947 Roswell incident, the report claims that witnesses obviously confused the chronology of events, erroneously thinking that the ambulances and bodies appeared at the same time. In other words, the witnesses really did see bodies (crash-test dummies or injured pilots and crew) and they did see ambulances, but years apart.

The Central Intelligence Agency (CIA) also released a report in 1997, both to provide explanations for UFO sightings and to clarify their own involvement over the years. Their report claims that a high percentage of UFOs were in fact CIA spyplanes, early on the U2 and later the SR71. As for sightings that predated these aircraft, the report supports theories of natural phenomena, other misidentifications, and agrees with the USAF's Project Mogul Balloon explanation of Roswell. Project Y receives minor (and incorrect) mention as a joint Canadian–British development. There is no discussion of the intense U.S. Army–U.S. Air Force involvement or of Project Silver Bug, nor is there any discussion of the 1956 joint American–Canadian agreements on the reporting of UFOs. The USAF report, the CIA report, and other critics of the Roswell incident have each pointed out that the story did not resurface until thirty years later, when UFO researchers began looking for witnesses.

Jack Litchfield, a former technician with the Canadian Broadcasting Corporation (CBC), has revealed exciting information that adds a new dimension to UFO studies. Litchfield told me that in 1950, Bill Richardson, then director of engineering at the CBC in Montreal, accompanied Wilbert Smith, the DOT employee and official of the Canadian government, to the North American Regional Broadcasting Conference in Washington, DC. During this trip, Smith made his "discreet" inquiries through the Canadian embassy that put him in touch with Dr. Sarbacher, ostensibly an official of the U.S. government. At this meeting, Dr. Sarbacher told Smith that flying saucers do exist, that they are not of this planet, and that a group of scientists headed by Dr. Vannevar Bush were studying them. Apparently unaware of Smith's meeting with Dr. Sarbacher, Bill Richardson somehow became convinced of the existence of UFOs. Unfortunately, it is not known who Richardson's sources were, but according to Litchfield, Richardson fully believed that American scientists were studying a recovered saucer.

Litchfield had read Donald Keyhoe's 1953 book, *Flying Saucers from Outer Space*, which makes considerable mention of Wilbert Smith, his work, and his beliefs in the interplanetary nature of UFOs. Bill Shearer, Litchfield's co-worker, was also well acquainted with Smith and his work, not just from Keyhoe's book, but also from his own contacts at the Canadian Defence Research Board (DRB). Litchfield and Shearer had a revealing meeting with Wilbert Smith on June 2, 1954. The two CBC technicians were involved in a site survey for a new transmitter in Ottawa when they decided to drop in on Smith. At the meeting, Smith spoke of his UFO detection and research station at Shirley's Bay. He told Litchfield and Shearer that he would be conducting tests at Shirley's Bay in the summer, but believed that the DRB would probably classify his project. Therefore, he feared his results would not be made public.

According to Litchfield, Shearer felt that Smith might have slipped up in commenting that the DRB might classify his tests and results. Shearer told Litchfield that the DRB was planning to take over Smith's project. Shearer offered several possible explanations for the takeover. He thought Smith might want out of the project because he was getting a bad reputation around Ottawa and some scientists were labelling him a crackpot. Also, Shearer thought Smith might have wanted out because the Department of Transport (DOT) was becoming embarrassed about Smith and his UFO involvement and public statements regarding his research work, including the UFO detection project. As I have pointed out in this book, the DOT was in fact embarrassed by the work, eventually forcing Smith to close down the UFO detection project.

Shearer further speculated that the DRB might be afraid that Smith would make his findings public. Shearer knew that Smith believed in keeping projects secret only in the interests of national security. So, according to Shearer, the DRB, concerned about any effects that the truth about the existence of flying saucers might have on the general public, would likely shroud the work and any results in secrecy, just as the USAF had done. Shearer's observations are most interesting, considering his contacts within the DRB. Personally, Shearer had nothing but the greatest respect for Wilbert Smith and declared categorically that Smith was not headed for "the loony bin," as a scientist friend of Shearer's had commented. Indeed, Smith went on to assume positions of higher authority in the Department of Transport.

One aspect of this meeting remains perplexing. Both Litchfield and Shearer were surprised by Smith's answer to their question about his belief in the interplanetary origin of flying saucers. Smith essentially told them that he no longer believed the saucers were interplanetary. He now felt the saucers existed in alternate universes, and he was developing mathematical calculations that he claimed showed the existence of these universes. (This theory of alternate universes is in fact supported more and more by some UFO researchers.) Smith also stated that contact with beings from these universes had been established through psychic means. In fact, in his inquiries in Washington in 1950, Smith had been told that U.S. authorities were investigating psychic research. Recalling that Bill Richardson believed American scientists were analyzing a crashed saucer, Litchfield asked Smith for his opinion. Smith replied he did not believe the saucers were being examined because the entities as he described them were not prepared to allow the examination of one of their craft. To the contrary, in later years Smith would state that he himself had analyzed pieces from flying saucers as early as 1952.

Perhaps he simply did not wish to divulge such information to Litchfield and Shearer.

Somewhat surprised at Smith's reply, Litchfield pressed for more information. Smith changed the subject and again spoke of contacting the UFOs' occupants through psychic means. He stated that a research group known as Borderland Research had published numerous papers on psychic research but that only some of their results were of any interest. (According to Curtis Peebles, author of *Watch the Skies*, Borderland Sciences Research Associates (BSRA) was an occult/contactee group that believed in a number of new-age concepts, including cosmic consciousness and prophecy.) A letter in the National Archives of Canada to Smith from BSRA, dated January 14, 1954, claims it was the BSRA who furnished Frank Scully with much of the information concerning the magnetic principles of the saucers' operation for his book *Behind the Flying Saucers*. The letter in the Archives also states that Scully then mistakenly credited this information to a mysterious and later discredited Dr. G. (Leo Gebauer). The letter also alleges BSRA had collaborative or cooperative contacts with others, including Kenneth Arnold and George Adamski, the latter being the famous or perhaps infamous contactee who claimed encounters with numerous beings from other worlds, but who others believed was only damaging the field with his fantastic tales.

Smith left the two CBC men with the impression that he no longer believed in the interplanetary nature of the saucers. In later years, though, he seems to have reverted to this thinking, evidenced by his claims of having physically handled pieces of saucers. What changed his mind, and why did he believe that the fragments he was receiving from authorities in the U.S. were legitimate?

According to Wilbert Smith's son, James, Smith did not necessarily change his mind. That is, he still believed in the idea of parallel or alternate universes, but he also believed in the interplanetary (or, more accurately, extraterrestrial) hypothesis. According to James Smith, on one of his many trips to the U.S. Wilbert Smith told his son that he was shown the bodies from a recovered craft. (This information has never before been made public, and James Smith makes it clear that his only proof of this claim is his father's word.) Wilbert Smith described the bodies as small and humanoid in appearance. James Smith does not recall any other details.

James Smith has kindly offered some additional insight into his father's other work. In this and the previous edition, I have written that Wilbert Smith had developed a device that he believed lost weight when activated. In other words, it levitated. Dr. Solandt advised me that the device never worked and any results were due to measurement error. James Smith says that what in fact levitated were objects placed above the device. The device itself was a circular coil less than twelve inches in diameter that produced a magnetic field. Specific details of the coil are not available, but James Smith believes the coil was rotated but is not certain if a rotating disc was mounted above the coil. When the device was activated, objects suspended above it were shown to lose weight.

This information is most intriguing in light of an article published in the December 1997 issue of *Popular Mechanics*. According to this article, National Aeronautics and Space Administration (NASA) researchers are in the process of studying possible anti-gravity effects. The set-up they have devised consists essentially of a superconducting ceramic disc, suspended and rotated above a magnetic field produced by three electric coils. Objects placed over the rotating disc are expected to lose weight, just as in Smith's experiments. Scientists believe that the rotating disc distorts gravity above it. This distortion of gravity is felt by some to be a by-product of Einstein's general theory of relativity. Researcher Dr. Ning Li of the University of Alabama, who is conducting this research for NASA, believes the superconducting ceramic disc serves to magnify the distortion effect.

The entire antigravity concept is based on the work of Dr. Eugene Podkletnov of Tampere University in Finland. According to Dr. Podkletnov, the effect was discovered while he was conducting routine work on superconductivity. His device consisted of a coil approximately 12 inches in diameter with a superconducting disc rotating above it at 5,000 revolutions per minute. Since news of the Podkletnov work has surfaced, others have claimed to have replicated the effect. Thus, NASA has decided to investigate further.

The *Popular Mechanics* article notes that many scientists believe the experiment will not work, and even if it does the effect would be too small to measure. In any event, the device looks similar to the one built by Wilbert Smith, and James Smith is quick to point out that information about his father's work was indeed sent to Tampere University. Whether the effect proves to be a true example of antigravity or some other phenomenon, it has already vindicated Wilbert Smith to some degree. If a true antigravity effect has been created, it may help explain the propulsive mechanisms behind UFOs that Smith was trying to determine.

In his conversations with me, James Smith also cleared up the controversy surrounding the death of his father, a subject that is much discussed on the Internet. Speculation abounds that Wilbert Smith died of brain cancer and that his death was somehow linked to his work with UFOs. It has also been suggested on the Internet that Wilbert died of stomach cancer. James has told me the truth — that Wilbert Smith died of lower bowel cancer December 27, 1962. He did not indicate whether he believed his father's death was related to UFO research.

With respect to the Michalak case, a new book, *UFOs: An Insider's View of the Official Quest for Evidence* (1997), by Dr. Roy Craig of the Condon Committee, reasserts the belief that Stefan Michalak hoaxed the entire episode. But he still fails to fully explain the physical evidence. Proponents of the extraterrestrial nature of the craft Michalak encountered still point to the physical evidence as proof the craft was from outer space. They note in particular Michalak's unusual symptoms following the encounter: nausea, vomiting, weight loss, and reduced lymphocyte count. They point out that some American doctors felt his reduced lymphocyte count was caused by exposure to high levels of radiation. What is not known, though, is what Michalak's lymphocyte count was just prior to the incident, for comparison purposes. The RCMP report notes that Michalak was not careful when handling suspected radioactive soil. It is possible that during some of his many forays into the woods, Michalak unknowingly exposed himself to high levels of naturally occurring radioactive substances that could have affected his lymphocyte count.

Although Michalak's story is contradictory in some respects, I do not believe that Stefan Michalak fabricated the incident. The RCMP agrees. However, I maintain there is nothing in his story that suggests what he saw was extraterrestrial in nature. Many who have experienced a close encounter note that the UFO sought them out. Michalak stated that he stumbled upon and surprised *the UFO* (though it is difficult to imagine that he could sneak up on beings normally associated with having telepathic abilities).

Michalak's encounter is not unlike that of police sergeant Lonnie Zamora. On April 24, 1964, Zamora was chasing a car on U.S. Highway 85 in Socorro, New Mexico. He was diverted from his pursuit by a roar and what appeared to be flames off to one side of the road. He proceeded on foot to investigate the noise and the flames. He saw an egg-shaped object on girder-like legs. Beside the object were two beings dressed in coveralls. As he approached them, he heard a noise, and flames erupted from the underside of the object, which took off and reached a height of about twenty feet. The noise stopped and the object hovered for a moment; it then flew off, but not before Zamora saw a red marking on the object's underside. Sergeant Chavez of the New Mexico State Police heard Zamora call for assistance. Chavez and Zamora found fresh marks in the soil where the craft had landed. The UFO Zamora described is different from the one that Michalak described. The propulsion system sounds rather conventional and several researchers suspect Zamora saw a terrestrial vehicle. Like Michalak, Zamora did not experience missing time or any of the other effects described by those who have reported close encounters, and Zamora came across the craft and its occupants, not the other way around.

Did Michalak and Zamora discover military crafts and not UFOs? The question remains unanswered. But research into military aircraft conducted by Jim Wilson, science editor of *Popular Mechanics*, shows that considerable effort went into the development of circular wing aircraft later on, after the completion of Project Silver Bug, the Canadian attempt to build a supersonic saucer. Included in this edition are some of the additional designs being studied by American companies when Avro was proposing Project Y (known to the CIA as Silver Bug).

In the National Archives of Canada is another previously unreported sighting from the 22nd NORAD region files. On December 16, 1976, off the northeastern coast of Canada, three KC-135 refueller aircraft and one C-5 aircraft were followed by an unknown object. The boom operator and navigator of one of the KC-135s reported that lights on the object were much brighter than the running lights on an aircraft. The object was about half a mile back and was 500 to 1,000 feet lower than the refuellers. In addition to this sighting, the object was picked up on the KC-135 radar. The UFO was not, however, picked up by ground radar. In fact, NORAD personnel were unaware that anything unusual had occurred during the refuelling operation. Five hours after the incident, Strategic Air Command (SAC) filed a report of the incident. NORAD wondered why the incident was not reported in progress. Had the report come in immediately, ground crew could have tried different means to track the object. In fact, NORAD had tracked only the four aircraft and did not notice anything out of the ordinary. If the UFO was in fact a secret military aircraft, it is unlikely that SAC would have reported the incident at all.

Hoax, secret aircraft, or extraterrestrial devices? The search for the truth continues.

Appendix: Selected Government Files

INTELLIGENCE - FLYING SAUCERS.

1.   DSI advised Secretary JIC on 6th April 1950 that the Minister had requested CDRB to seek the co-operation of the Services in reporting on the occurrences or alleged occurrences of Flying Saucers passing over Canada. He requested that this be discussed at the next meeting of the JIC.

2.   This was discussed at the 220th meeting of the JIC which took place on 12th April 1950. Paras 19,20 and 21 of the Minutes are as follows:-

19. Mr. Langley reported that the Minister of National Defence had requested that the Chairman of the Defence Research Board seek the co-operation of the Services in reporting on the occurrences or alleged occurrences of flying saucers passing over Canada.

A number of cases had been reported in various parts of Canada and it was suggested that the field intelligence officers of the three Services and the Royal Canadian Mounted Police might be instructed to investigate these incidents and report thereon to the Department of National Defence. Such reports could be dealt with ultimately either by the Directorate of Air Intelligence or the Directorate of Scientific Intelligence.

20. Colonel Todd suggested that the Director of Air Intelligence and the Director of Scientific Intelligence might be asked to collaborate in the preparation of a suitable questionnaire which could be circulated to the intelligence officers and the Royal Canadian Mounted Police in the field to assist them in their investigations.

21. The Committee, after further discussion, agreed that:

(a) the Director of Air Intelligence and the Director of Scientific Intelligence collaborate in the preparation of a questionnaire suitable for investigating and reporting upon the occurrences or alleged occurrences of flying saucers passing over Canada;

(b) these questionnaires be distributed to field intelligence officers of the three services and to the Royal Canadian Mounted Police to assist them in their investigations;

(c) the Director of Air Intelligence co-ordinate the investigation arrangements in the field as between the three Services and the Royal Canadian Mounted Police; and

(d) all the field reports on flying saucers be passed to the Director of Scientific Intelligence for final examination on behalf of the Department of National Defence.

...........·/2

Canada's Department of National Defence decides to take the question of flying saucers seriously, at a time when it is being discounted in the United States.
— *National Archives of Canada*

3.   DSI prepared a preliminary draft questionnaire and forwarded it to DAI, ref. letter DRBS 200-4-160 (DSI) dated 19th April 1950. Paras 4 and 5 of DSI's letter suggested that completed questionnaires are to be forwarded immediately to DAI and in the case of a Flying Saucer actually landing on Canadian territory that the nearest RCAF Command should be advised immediately.

4.   DAI forwarded to DSI under cover of their memorandum S 21-1-9 (DAI) dated 30 August 1950 a revised questionnaire submitted for DSI's consideration. At that time DAI advised that if the questionnaire was approved, copies would be forwarded to the various Army, Navy and Air Force Commands for implementation. Necessary instructions to the Commandes would be given as to the questions outlined in paras 4 and 5 of DSI's letter.

Sept. 15–1950

Notes on interview through A/C.
Bremner with Dr. Robert J Sarbacher.

WBS: I am doing some work on the
collapse of the earth's magnetic
field as a source of energy,
and I think our work may
have a bearing on the flying
Saucers.

RJS What do you want to know.

WBS I have read Scully's book on
the saucers and would like
to know how much of it is
true.

RJS The facts reported in the book are
substantially correct.

WBS Then the saucers do exist?

RJS Yes they exist.

WBS Do they operate as Scully
suggests on magnetic
principles?

Wilbert Smith's notes from his September 1950 meeting with American
scientist Dr. Robert Sarbacher, in which Sarbacher tells him that flying saucers
are real. — *Arthur Bray Collection*

RLS. We have not been able to duplicate their performance

WBS Do they come from some other planet?

RLS All we know is, we didn't make them, and it's pretty certain they didn't originate on the earth.

WBS I understand the whole subject of saucers is classified

RLS. Yes, it is classified two points higher even than the H-bomb. In fact it is the most highly classified subject in the US Government at the present time.

WBS May I ask the reason for the classification?

RLS You may ask, but I can't tell you

WDS: Is there any way in which I can get more information, particularly as it might fit in with our own work.

RLS: I suppose you could be cleared through your own Defense Department and I am pretty sure arrangements could be made to exchange information. If you have anything to contribute, we would be glad to talk it over, but I can't give you any more at the present time.

Note: The above is written out from memory following the interview. I have tried to keep it as nearly verbatim as possible.

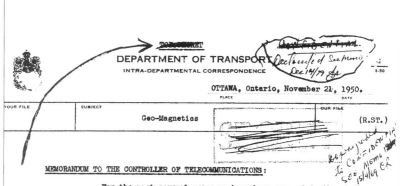

DEPARTMENT OF TRANSPORT
INTRA-DEPARTMENTAL CORRESPONDENCE

OTTAWA, Ontario, November 21, 1950.

PLACE   DATE

YOUR FILE	SUBJECT		OUR FILE	
	Geo-Magnetics			(R.ST.)

MEMORANDUM TO THE CONTROLLER OF TELECOMMUNICATIONS:

For the past several years we have been engaged in the study of various aspects of radio wave propagation. The vagaries of this phenomenon have led us into the fields of aurora, cosmic radiation, atmospheric radio-activity and geo-magnetism. In the case of geo-magnetics our investigations have contributed little to our knowledge of radio wave propagation as yet, but nevertheless have indicated several avenues of investigation which may well be explored with profit. For example, we are on the track of a means whereby the potential energy of the earth's magnetic field may be abstracted and used.

On the basis of theoretical considerations a small and very crude experimental unit was constructed approximately a year ago and tested in our Standards Laboratory. The tests were essentially successful in that sufficient energy was abstracted from the earth's field to operate a volt-meter, approximately 50 milliwatts. Although this unit was far from being self-sustaining, it nevertheless demonstrated the soundness of the basic principles in a qualitative manner and provided useful data for the design of a better unit.

The design has now been completed for a unit which should be self-sustaining and in addition provide a small surplus of power. Such a unit, in addition to functioning as a 'pilot power plant' should be large enough to permit the study of the various reaction forces which are expected to develop.

We believe that we are on the track of something which may well prove to be the introduction to a new technology. The existence of a different technology is borne out by the investigations which are being carried on at the present time in relation to flying saucers.

While in Washington attending the NARB Conference, two books were released, one titled "Behind the Flying Saucer" by Frank Scully, and the other "The Flying Saucers are Real" by Donald Keyhoe. Both books dealt mostly with the sightings of unidentified objects and both books claim that flying objects were of extra-terrestrial origin and might well be space ships

...... 2

Smith advises his superiors at the Canadian Ministry of Transport that flying saucers exist and are being studied in the United States by Dr. Vannevar Bush.
— *National Archives of Canada*

from another planet. Scully claimed that the preliminary studies of
one saucer which fell into the hands of the United States Government
indicated that they operated on some hitherto unknown magnetic
principles. It appeared to me that our own work in geo-magnetics
might well be the linkage between our technology and the technology
by which the saucers are designed and operated. If it is assumed that
our geo-magnetic investigations are in the right direction, the theory
of operation of the saucers becomes quite straightforward, with all
observed features explained qualitatively and quantitatively.

I made discreet enquiries through the Canadian Embassy
staff in Washington who were able to obtain for me the following
information:

a. The matter is the most highly classified subject in the United
   States Government, rating higher even than the H-bomb.

b. Flying saucers exist.

c. Their modus operandi is unknown but concentrated effort is being
   made by a small group headed by Doctor Vannevar Bush.

d. The entire matter is considered by the United States authorities
   to be of tremendous significance.

I was further informed that the United States authorities are investigating
along quite a number of lines which might possibly be related to the saucers
such as mental phenomena and I gather that they are not doing too well since
they indicated that if Canada is doing anything at all in geo-magnetics they
would welcome a discussion with suitably accredited Canadians.

While I am not yet in a position to say that we have solved
even the first problems in geo-magnetic energy release, I feel that the
correlation between our basic theory and the available information on
saucers checks too closely to be mere coincidence. It is my honest opinion
that we are on the right track and are fairly close to at least some of the
answers.

Mr. Wright, Defence Research Board liaison officer at the
Canadian Embassy in Washington, was extremely anxious for me to get in touch
with Doctor Solandt, Chairman of the Defence Research Board, to discuss with
him future investigations along the line of geo-magnetic energy release.

.... 3

I do not feel that we have as yet sufficient data to place before Defence Research Board which would enable a program to be initiated within that organization, but I do feel that further research is necessary and I would prefer to see it done within the frame work of our own organization with, of course, full co-operation and exchange of information with other interested bodies.

I discussed this matter fully with Doctor Solandt, Chairman of Defence Research Board, on November 20th and placed before him as much information as I have been able to gather to date. Doctor Solandt agreed that work on geo-magnetic energy should go forward as rapidly as possible and offered full co-operation of his Board in providing laboratory facilities, acquisition of necessary items of equipment, and specialized personnel for incidental work in the project. I indicated to Doctor Solandt that we would prefer to keep the project within the Department of Transport for the time being until we have obtained sufficient information to permit a complete assessment of the value of the work.

It is therefore recommended that a PROJECT be set up within the frame work of this Section to study this problem and that the work be carried on a part time basis until such time as sufficient tangible results can be seen to warrant more definitive action. Cost of the program in its initial stages are expected to be less than a few hundred dollars and can be carried by our Radio Standards Lab appropriation.

Attached hereto is a draft of terms of reference for such a project which, if authorized, will enable us to proceed with this research work within our own organization.

(W.B. Smith)
Senior Radio Engineer

WBS/CC

Air Services
Telecommunications Division

OTTAWA, Ontario, January 3, 1951.

Dear Gordon:

I would like to bring you up to date in our magnetic program and also request from you any information which you have been able to obtain along these lines since we last discussed the matter.

We have three engineers working full time on the program, together with two technicians, with concentrated effort on the magnetic sink. Progress is, of necessity, slow because of the physical labour involved in making the various set-ups and measurements necessary.

Full co-operation is being given by Defence Research Board and National Research Council although at this stage in the work there is not a great deal that they can do beyond assisting in some of the machine work and providing materials and instruments. The holiday season of course made quite a hole in our program as no one felt inclined to put forth a maximum effort at that time.

I understand that Doctor Solandt was in Washington for sometime recently but I have not had a chance to speak to him since he returned. I do not think that he uncovered anything of significance or he would have passed the information along to us. It is possible that Mr. Wright may be able to add something.

Incidentally, our program is now official within the Department of Transport and is known as Project Magnet. It is classified as secret until such time as we know where we stand. Doctor Solandt has requested that we respect fully the United States classification on these matters.

Doctor Solandt referred Donald Keyhoe's draft article to me for comment. I took extreme exception to the first portion of the article which dealt with material which we had discussed, and in order to preserve our position I took the liberty of redrafting the first part of this article.

.... 2

A letter from Smith to Gordon Cox, an official at the Canadian Embassy in Washington. Smith notes that Project Magnet, a secret Canadian UFO propulsion research project, is now official. — *Arthur Bray Collection*

I returned the article with the revision to Doctor Solandt together with
a letter to Keyhoe explaining my action. I also asked Doctor Solandt
to show the article revision and letter to the others in our group for
their comments and any further revisions which they might consider in
Canadian interests.

I have heard nothing further in regard to the Keyhoe article
and I was wondering if you could throw any light on the subject. I imagine
that it has long since been returned to the Canadian Embassy in Washington
after which I understand Keyhoe was to take it to Doctor Bush for clearance.
I do not know what Doctor Bush's reaction will be to the material contained
in the major portion of the article and my revision, but his reaction
should certainly be interesting and I would like you to have a talk with
Keyhoe sometime at your convenience to ascertain this point.

I trust that you had a completely satisfactory Yuletide season
and kept up the tradition of Canadians in Washington.

Yours sincerely,

(W.B. Smith)

CANADIAN EMBASSY
AMBASSADE DU CANADA

SECRET   1746 Massachusetts Avenue, N.W.,
                                Washington 6, D. C.

                                January 6, 1951

        Dear Wilbert,

                Thank you for your letter of January 3. I
        was glad to hear how well you were progressing with
        arrangements for Project Magnet and I hope that this
        will give you ample opportunity to proceed with your
        research.

                There is very little more that can be done
        here for the present. The official position is still
        that nobody knows anything about the matter here at
        all. We are, of course, keeping our ears and eyes
        open and if anything does develop you will probably
        hear through the Wright and Solandt channel. On the
        Ambassador's instructions no one in the Embassy, apart
        from Wright and myself, is to discuss the matter with
        anyone.

                I shall be glad, of course, to act as a
        post office and I think it would be useful to keep
        this channel open.

                I have not yet had an opportunity to meet
        Keyhoe but I can easily do so through Bremner, and
        I will make an exploratory contact in the near future.
        I did not see his article after it was referred to you.
        I can appreciate your annoyance with the first two or

                                                    ... 2.

W.D. Smith, Esq.,
  Air Services,
    Telecommunications Division,
      Department of Transport,
        Ottawa, Canada.

A letter from Cox to Smith in 1951, advising him that, officially, no one at the
Canadian Embassy knows anything. — *Arthur Bray Collection*

three paragraphs. The article was returned to Keyhoe
through Wright and he has not seen it since nor has
he heard anything from Bush or what Bush did. I may
be able to get something more on this angle after
seeing Keyhoe.

Is it possible to get "True" in Canada or
should I send you a copy when and if the article comes
out?

The Ambassador and I would be particularly
interested in any indication you may have heard when
you were here on the possibility of an official U.S.
Government statement. It is this political angle with
which I will be principally concerned. Anything you
can do to help in this respect will be welcome.

There are a number of matters which I would
like to discuss with you and if I manage to get up to
Ottawa anytime in the next month or so I will make a
point of getting in touch with you.

Thanks very much for your Christmas card. I
hope that your celebrations were as alcoholic as ours.

Yours sincerely,

Gordon E. Cox.

DRBC 260-4-45(Aero)

94

DEFENCE RESEARCH BOARD

PROJECT SECOND STOREY

Minutes of the 2/52 Meeting

CGS BOARD ROOM, OTTAWA 6267
19th May, 1952

Chairman:	Dr. P.M. Millman	Dom. Observ.
Members:	Lt. Cdr. J.C. Annesely	DNI
	S/L L.P.S. Bing	JIS
	F/L V.L. Bradley	DRB
	Maj.D.M. Grant	DMI
	Lt.Col. E.H. Webb	DMO&P
	Mr. W.B. Smith	DOT
Secretary:	Mr. H.C. Oatway	DRB

The Minutes of the first meeting of the Committee 24 April 1952 were considered and, with some minor changes approved. These have been reproduced and distributed.

A correction to the minutes of the general meeting 22nd April 1952 was tabled as follows:

Page 2, last para to read:

"It was decided that a Committee should be formed to give a lead in this activity and to standardize procedures, etc. Accordingly the following were nominated and agreed to act: Dr. Millman (Chairman) G/C Edwards, Lt. Col. Webb, Cdr Pratt, F/L Bradley, and Mr. W.B. Smith, and Mr. Oatway (Secretary).

This committee was to prepare a brief of instructions for observers; examine interrogation procedures and to get a consolidated and pertinent series of questions: "

With reference a communication from the Chairman of the Defence Research Board, Dr. Millman cautioned the members with respect to dealing with the press and public. The committee and all deliberations are classified as Confidential and must be so treated. Contacts with the press or public are not to be made.

The last meeting considered that the name Project Theta would be desirable for this project and Committee, providing it would no duplicate an existing project name, or contravene regulations. The Secretary pointed out that the word "theta" has not been assigned to Canada under tripartite agreements. Additionally, if a single word name were used, it as well as the Committee deliberations, would be classed as Confidential and could not appear on interrogation forms which would be used to obtain data from the public. Any two-word name may be used openly and as such is known as a nickname. Nicknames may be used for classified projects. The Committee then agreed to the name "Project Second Storey".

In 1952, Project Second Storey is formed. Although the name was chosen so that it would appear on forms used in obtaining data from the public, no contact with the press or public was to be made. — *National Archives of Canada*

INTRA-DEPARTMENTAL CORRESPONDENCE

OTTAWA, Ontario. June 10, 1954.
PLACE   DATE

YOUR FILE	SUBJECT	OUR FILE

MEMORANDUM TO SUPERINTENDENT OF RADIO REGULATIONS

1.   Pursuant to our conversation regarding the status of Project Magnet, may I bring the following to your attention.

2.   I am satisfied that there is a sufficient probability for the real existence of some Unidentified Flying Objects as Alien Vehicles, to warrant carrying on with the investigations and if possible, expanding them to include a more intensive study of the physics of the problem.

3.   Whether or not these studies continue within the purview of this Division, I certainly intend to carry on with them. I feel that there is much to be learned in this field and that I would be most remiss if I did not follow up the leads I have.

4.   I realize that this subject can hardly be considered as a Telecommunications matter, and for this reason I would suggest one of the following courses of action:

    (a)   To re-establish Project Magnet within Transport but outside of the Telecommunications Division, as a separate project.

    (b)   To provide a nominal grant for the continuation of the project on a spare time basis

    (c)   To release the project entirely from this Department so that it may be carried on as a private effort.

5.   I would point out that only the first two methods permit government control of the work, or the disposition of results, and for this reason it would appear desirable to work out something along these lines.

C.T. as you are aware I am not in agreement with para. 2. Alternative 4 c. would seem preferable but it raises the issue of a Civil Servant & private publicity. Z H memo of 23 March '54 refers. Kindly advise.
LR 14.6.54

..........2

In a memorandum to his superiors, Smith reiterates his belief that UFOs are alien vehicles; his boss, Mr. C. M. Brant, disagrees in a handwritten note at bottom. — *National Archives of Canada*

DEPARTMENT OF TRANSPORT
INTRA-DEPARTMENTAL CORRESPONDENCE

2
4-52

Ottawa, 25th June, 1954.

YOUR FILE	SUBJECT	OUR FILE
	Projects Magnet and Second Storey	2212-33 Secret 22-12-29 " (CT)

MEMORANDUM TO SUPT.OF RADIO REGULATIONS:

1. I am returning, herewith, your memorandum of April 27th, with attachments, also Mr.Smith's memorandum to you of the 10th instant.

2. You will recall that we had a preliminary discussion on these with the D.M.A., at which time it was decided that action should be deferred until the latter had had an opportunity to review the whole question with Dr.Solandt.

3. Mr.Baldwin has now informed me that he has discussed the matter with Dr.Solandt and has advised me as follows,-

> Dr.Solandt stated that he has checked around and was of the opinion that no facts had emerged which would warrant making this a special government project. As far as he has been able to find out, both here and in the United States, as well as in the United Kingdom, no special research is going on. In the circumstances he agreed with the viewpoint I then expressed to him, namely, that Mr.Smith should be told that so far as official work is concerned, this project must not be carried on in Departmental time, and that what he wishes to do in his own free time is purely a matter for himself; also that, as heretofore, we will not refuse him access to use of equipment that we are not using for our own purposes, and which is available, but that any work done from here on will not be done under any official Departmental sponsorship.
> Dr.Solandt's own investigations with the D.R.B. personnel indicate that they do not, from their own knowledge of what is going on here and in Washington, consider it worthwhile putting any further top level people on the investigation in the sense that Mr.Smith had earlier wanted as desirable.
> That in the event of Mr.Smith's name being coupled officially with the Department in any publicity, that might eventually develop through his spare time investigation, the Department would have to take the position publicly that there was no official Departmental sponsorship of Mr.Smith's activities.

4. Will you kindly inform Mr.Smith accordingly.

(G.C.W.Browne)
Controller of Telecommunications

GCWB:EWS

cc- Mr. van Allen.

Recommendations are made to distance the Department of Transport and the Defence Research Board from Smith's UFO research. — *National Archives of Canada*

FOR EARLY WARNING IN DEFENCE OF THE NORTH AMERICAN CONTINENT

CIRVIS-MERINT REPORTING PROCEDURE

1. MESSAGE IDENTIFICATION

(a) Reports made from airborne and land-based sources will be identified by CIRVIS (pronounced SUR-VEES) as the first word of the text.

(b) Reports made by waterborne sources will be identified by MERINT (pronounced MUR-ENT) as the first word of the text.

2. WHAT TO REPORT

Report immediately all airborne and waterborne objects which appear to be HOSTILE, are UNIDENTIFIED or are acting suspiciously.

Submarines, surfaced or partly submerged.

Surface warships positively identified as not Canadian or U.S. Other ships or boats acting suspiciously.

Aircraft or vapour trails which appear to be directed against Canada, the United States, their territories or possessions.

Guided Missiles

Unidentified Flying Objects or unidentified objects in the water.

3. SEND TO ANY

Canadian Military Establishment,
RCMP Post,
Department of Transport or Fisheries Representative,
Hudson's Bay Company Northern Radio-Equipped Store, or
The nearest open Canadian Telegraph Office. (By telephone if necessary.)
Use the quickest possible means to make your report.

4. SEND THIS KIND OF MESSAGE

(a) Begin your message with the word "CIRVIS" or "MERINT" as applicable.
(b) Give the identification of the observer, aircraft or vessel making the report.
(c) Describe briefly the objects sighted.
(d) Indicate where and when the objects were sighted.
(e) If objects are airborne, estimate altitude as "low", "medium", "high".
(f) Give direction of travel of sighted objects.
(g) Estimate and give speed of sighted objects.
(h) Give other significant information.

5. SEND IMMEDIATELY

DO NOT DELAY YOUR REPORT DUE TO INCOMPLETE INFORMATION.

NOTE

There are no charges to the originator in the handling of CIRVIS or MERINT messages.

Authorised by Department of National Defence
Authorised for display in Post Offices by the Postmaster General

From this 1950s Department of National Defence poster there is no mistaking what is meant by a UFO. — *National Archives of Canada*

MEMORANDUM

10 Dec 57

ACAS.

Unidentified Flying Objects

1   Reference the request from the Under Secretary of State for External Affairs on behalf of the High Commissioner at London, dated 27 Nov 57.

2   The RCAF has no official policy concerning the subject. There is no office within NDHQ commissioned to deal with the reports of these phenomena, although DAI seems to be the gathering place for them. There is a recorded instance in October 1950, where A/C Bryans, then AMAP, ordered that reports would be filed, but that investigations would be played down. There has never been a serious investigation of any report on file at AFHQ.

3   The Chief of the Radio Division in the Department of Transport, Mr. W.B. Smith, (against the advice of his superiors) has had himself appointed chairman to the Canadian Committee of the National Investigations Committee on Aerial Phenomena, headquartered at Washington, DC. It would seem that External Affairs should be directed to Mr. W.B. Smith for the answers they seek.

4   A memorandum to this effect for DM's signature is attached.

(R.B. Ingalls) G/C
Director of Air Intelligence

Att

The RCAF denies having interest in or a policy concerning UFOs. — *National Archives of Canada*

3940-105(CAS)
~~810-12(CAS)~~

MEMORANDUM

Ref Parliamentary Returns No 2340
              dated 21 Oct 63   OCT 2 3 1963

Parliamentary Returns Section

Reply to Question No 1,416

1   The following information is submitted in response to
question 1,416 raised by Mr Winch:

   (a) Para 1. Canada co-operates with the United
        States for the investigation of reports of
        unidentified flying objects. If a report
        warrants investigation, the investigation is
        conducted by Air Defence Command. In the
        normal course of events NORAD Headquarters would
        receive a copy of the report. Such investiga-
        tions are not entitled "Project Magnet" and, in
        fact, no codename is applied to reports of un-
        identified flying objects.

   (b) Para 2. "Project Magnet" was the brain child of
        the late Wilbert B Smith of the Department of
        Transport, a project which he carried on in his
        own time without Government financial support.
        Because the records of "Project Magnet" were
        never made available to the Department of National
        Defence, nothing is known about their equipment
        or personnel.

   (c) Para 3. Wilbert B Smith was employed in the Radio
        Regulations Division of the Department of Transport,
        and was the head of a UFO research project which
        he conducted as a personal undertaking.

   (d) Para 4. Files and data compiled under "Project
        Magnet" - if any - are not controlled by Depart-
        ment of National Defence, therefore, availability
        of such data to the general public cannot be
        stated.

                              ORIGINAL SIGNED BY
                              (W. M. GARTON) G/C
                              A/CAS

                              (C.R. Dunlap)
                              Air Marshal
                              Chief of the Air Staff

The RCAF admits to co-operating in the investigation of UFOs but distances
itself from Smith — despite his backing from the Defence Research Board.
— *National Archives of Canada*

REPORTING OF UNIDENTIFIED FLYING OBJECTS

GENERAL

1.   Reports of unidentified flying objects (UFOs) are frequently received at Canadian Forces bases from various sources. CFHQ is responsible for processing any action required on these reports. Accordingly, UFO reports shall be transmitted to CFHQ in accordance with para 2.

REPORTING

2.   Unclassified priority messages shall be addressed to CANFORCEHED and the first words in the text shall be "FOR CFOC. UFO REPORT". All reports shall include as much of the following information as is obtainable, using the identifying letter indicated:

A   Date and time of sighting (GMT).

B   Condition of sky (clear, cloudy, haze, etc).

C   Identification of observer.

D   Location of observer at time of sighting.

E   Identification of other persons also observing the UFO.

F   Description of sighting (shape, colour, altitude, movement, number of UFOs, etc).

G   Duration of observation.

H   Any other relevant information.

3.   Fireball and meteorite observations shall be reported in accordance with with CFAO 71-1

                                                                S 1605-71-6
(C)   V 2000-4 (DOPS)

Issued 7 Oct 66

Indexing
Unidentified Flying Objects
Reports & Returns

                                                                AL 40/66

This Canadian Forces Administrative Order (CFAO 71-6) was issued in 1966 for the reporting of UFOs. Note the existence of a separate order (CFAO 71-1) for fireballs and meteorites. — *National Archives of Canada*

Ottawa 4, Ontario
February 16, 1968

The Honourable L. Cadieux
Minister of National Defence
125 Elgin Street
Ottawa 4, Ontario

My dear Colleague:

Subject to your concurrence, I can now confirm that the National Research Council has agreed to act as the repository of reports of unidentified flying objects.

Therefore, if you agree, your existing file of such reports, as well as any which may be received in the future by your Department, may be forwarded to the Radio and Electrical Engineering Division of NRC. Your Department should retain any reports which it is felt should be classified for reasons of military security.

Investigations by NRC, if any, of these reports will depend on the degree of scientific interest in each case. Officials of your Department and of NRC have collaborated in similar examinations in the past, and their continued cooperation would be most appreciated.

Yours sincerely,

C. M. Drury

In 1968, the National Research Council agrees to take over the collection of UFO reports, but notes that DND should retain any reports that it feels "should be classified for reasons of military security." — *National Archives of Canada*

HEADQUARTERS QUARTIER GENERAL
CANADIAN FORCES FIGHTER GROUP/CANADIAN NORAD REGION
GROUPE DE CHASSE DES FORCES CANADIENNES/REGION CANADIENNE DU NORAD
HORNELL HEIGHTS, ONTARIO P0H 1P0

G2075-5 (SSO FCAS)

27 September 1988

Commanding Officer
Radar Control Wing
Hornell Heights, Ont
POH 1PO

REPORTING ATMOSPHERIC PHENOMENA (UFO/METEOR)

1.   The deletion of CFAO 71-1 has apparently caused some confusion about the procedures to be followed for the reporting of Atmospheric Phenomena. This letter is written to clarify any such uncertainties.

2.   The National Defence Operations Centre (NDOC) Ottawa no longer chooses to receive UFO/METEOR reports hence the deletion of CFAO 71-1. However, these reports are still required by all other addressees previously listed in WING OI 2.110. These addressees are Air Command Operations Centre Winnipeg, NORAD Cheyenne Mtn Complex CO/J3Y, FGHQ North Bay/SSO Int, and NRC Ottawa for Meteor Centre or NRC Ottawa for Herzberg Institute of Astrophysics in the case of a UFO report.

3.   The procedures previously adhered to were sufficient for the reporting of atmospheric phenomena. Therefore, with the exception of deleting NDOC Ottawa as an addressee from WING OI 2.110, all procedures outlined therein should remain unchanged.

2 WORSO
for your action
4/10

D.A. McEwan
Lieutenant-Colonel
for Commander

It is clear that the Department of National Defence remains interested in receiving UFO reports. — *National Archives of Canada*

AIR TRAFFIC CONTROL LOG BOOK

22 U.R. FACILITY   DATE 11/11 19 75

TIME	DETAILS	ENTERED BY
1118	CFB FALCONBRIDGE (M.K.) CALLED RE UFO. OVER THE BASE AND ALSO REP OF UFO OVER OPP BLDG DOWNTOWN SUDBURY. BRILLIANT COLOR LIKE LOOKING AT A LARGE GEM WITH COLORED LIGHTS ALL AROUND IT.	'14
1123	NORTH CAPE ACTIVITY - INTEL O (MAJ LITTLE) STAND-BY DO (COL OECHSLE) ADVISED	14
1147	MAJ OLIVER FM FALCONBRIDGE CALLED RE UFO'S. REPORT IS AS FOLLOWS TIME 1152 - 1129Z - SIGHTED 2 UFO BRILLIANT LIGHTS - ONE AT 200° FM CFB FALCONBRIDGE, THE OTHER AT 180° BUT MUCH FURTHER AWAY. MAJ OLIVER TOOK 3 SNAP SHOTS WITH BROWNIE CAMERA (NO RESULTS) AS OF THIS TIME. OTHER OBSERVERS WERE CAPT CARSON AND CPL LAWRENCESON OF CFB FALCONBRIDGE — THEY OBSERVE THE CLOSEST OBJECT THROUGH BINOCULARS AND OBJECT WAS RISING VERTICALLY AT TREMENDOUS SPEED - THEY HAD IT ON HT FINDER AT TWO CUTS OF 44,000' AND AGAIN AT 72,000' - OBJECT CIRCULAR - WELL LIGHTED AND AND WHAT APPEARED AS TWO BLACK SPOTS IN THE CENTRE.	/1

NORAD SAFE KEY 1 - TEAM "A" CF OFF/SR [signature]

NORAD SAFE KEY 2 - TEAM "B" US OFF/SR NCO Harold A. Scott

SD A ON DUTY [signature]

SD B OFF DUTY [signature]   TIME 12.04

TIME	DETAILS	ENTERED BY
1231	WARSHIP: DTG 11/1023 TRACK II ONE FADED POSITION 67.30N. 005.00E @ 11/1152 NOTIFIED COL OECHSLEY + MAJ. LITTLE	HL
1303	STARTOVER CONT. TO INSERT IO OCTALS. AF	HL
1310	WARSHIP - DTG 11/1023 TRACK II ONE REAPPEARED 64.00N, 001.00N, ONE UK F-4 SCRAMBLED. 1235.	HL
1322	22ND RCC NOW ON COMMERCIAL POWER.	HL

In 1975, observers at Canadian Forces Base Falconbridge tracked a UFO on height finder radar, first at 44,000 feet, then at 72,000 feet, rising at tremendous speed. Media reports gave the misleading impression that the altitudes were merely guessed at by witnesses. — *National Archives of Canada*

C O P Y   M E M O R A N D U M   RESTRICTED

S.21-1-9 (DAI)
4 Aug 50

Secretary,
Joint Intelligence Committee.

Classification cancelled / Changed to ....
By authority of ....
Date ....
Signature ....
Unit / Rank / Appointment ....

Flying Saucers

1   At the 220th meeting on April 12th it was agreed (Item VI)
that DSI and DAI should prepare a questionnaire for investigating and
reporting upon the occurrences of flying saucers passing over Canada.
About that time the USAF publicly announced that they had stopped
investigating sighting reports and had wound up project "Saucer". An
officer of this Directorate proceeded to Washington and examined the
special study which had been written on completion of the project.
This study indicated that the sightings were either natural phenomena,
hoaxes or imaginary, and concluded that no foreign or extraterrestrial
aircraft were involved in any of the incidents. It was apparent too
that on every occasion where publicity attended such sightings there
were innumerable further sighting reports immediately afterwards. The
present USAF policy is to play down the subject, investigating only
when considered necessary by the area commander without any special
arrangements for reporting or investigation.

2   It seems that a similar policy on our part would be wise
and that it would be undesirable to produce a special questionnaire
or make any arrangements for investigation since this would tend to
give publicity to the matter. It is suggested therefore that sighting
reports should not be solicited and such as are volunteered should be
passed to DSI for retention and further action only if such action
seems necessary.

3   It may perhaps be advisable to have this matter brought up
in committee so that an official decision can be taken.

(Sgd.)   G.S. Austin

W/C
Acting DAI

A memo from the Acting Director of Air Intelligence (DAI) to the Secretary of the Joint Intelligence Committee. Despite the misgivings of the DAI, as outlined in paragraph two, the Joint Intelligence Committee, acting on a request from the Minister of National Defence, developed a questionnaire for various field offices to use when interrogating witnesses of sightings and began investigating UFOs.
— *National Archives of Canada*

M E M O R A N D U M

8 October, 1958.

Mr. Stannard:

Investigations of Unidentified Flying Objects

1.   Reference your minute re letter from the National Investigations Committee on Aerial Phenomena dated 14 August, 1958. I have drawn up a draft letter which PRO might forward to NICAP. It should be noted that Mr. Smith is a member of this organization and surely the Director of NICAP must be aware of this. It was also thought that the procedure for investigations of UFO reports should be reviewed to establish what was now being done by Canadian agencies in this regard.

2.   **Past History**

     U.S. "Project Saucer" was completed about 1950 and it was found desirable to solicit Canadian reports. At the 220th meeting of the JIC on the 12, Apr. 1950, UFO's were discussed and the following decisions were reached:

         (a)   DSI and DAI were to collaborate in preparing a questionnaire to be distributed to field intelligence officers of the three services and the RCMP.

         (b)   DAI is to co-ordinate the investigation arrangements in the field.

         (c)   All field reports were to be passed to DSI for official examination on behalf of DND.

In late 1950 a questionnaire or sighting report form was drawn up and approved; copies and instructions were passed to field units. (Ref: letter S21-1-9 (DAI) 19 October, 1950 to TCHQ)

3.   In 1952 the "Project Second Story" Committee was formed and the sighting report form was revised. The Committee met about six times, the most recent meeting apparently being 25 Feb. 54. The Committee concluded its activities which were summarized in a memo by Dr. Millman, Chairman. It was concluded that the sightings did not lend themselves to a scientific method of investigation. In 1954 the Secretary of the Committee informed DAI of Dr. Millman's summary and stated that reports were still being collected, but that no analysis was being carried out.

4.   **Action by DRB/DSI**

     A tabular record of reports of sightings dating back to 1954 was initiated by F/L Birch of DSI. This is kept in this office and is classified SECRET. The last entry is a sighting of 8th June 1956. A file is also kept here which contains a multitude of press articles, sightings, etc. DRB file 3800-10-1-1 (3 vols.) contains a large number of sighting reports dating back to 1947.

5.   **Recent Action by DAI**

     This morning I examined a number of files held in DAI and talked to S/L Lovelace. In January, 1957 DAI initiated liaison duties with Mr. W. Smith of the Department of Transport. A sighting report form was devised which proved to be identical to that devised by Project Second Story Committee. A copy of this form is attached.

6.   In December, 1957 a letter was prepared by DAI in reply to a request from a magazine regarding Canadian policy in investigating UFO's. An extract is as follows: "The DND makes no provision for the investigation into these phenomena. However, it has come to our attention that Mr. W.B.

A DRB memo to a Mr. Stannard, suggesting that various field offices, including the RCMP, may have carried out some investigations of sightings in 1950. I have not been able to find any of the results of these investigations. The secret tabular listing of UFO sightings mentioned in paragraph four is unavailable. Paragraph

Smith, Chief of Radio Division DOT Room 2210, No. 8 Temporary Building, has made and is making extensive studies on the subject of UFO's. Mr. Smith is ex-officio Canadian Chairman of NICAP located in Washington, D.C." The letter was signed by the Deputy Minister for National Defence.

7.   Also in December, 1957 a letter was written to ACAS by DAI: "The RCAF has no official policy concerning the subject. There is no office within NDHQ commissioned to deal with the reports of these phenomena, although DAI seems to be a gathering place for them. There has been a recorded instance of October, 1950 where A/C Brians, then AMAP, ordered that reports would be filed, but that investigations would be played down. There has never been an investigation of any report on file at AFHQ". (Ref: C940-105 (DAI) 10th December, 1957)

8.   At present, S/L Lovelace in DAI deals with the matter of flying saucers and is maintaining liaison with Mr. Smith. If a report is received the observer is asked by DAI to complete a sighting report form which is then forwarded to Mr. Smith. The last report in the DAI files was dated July, 1958. DAI did not appear to be aware of earlier policy as explained in paragraphs 2 and 3 above.

9.   It would appear that DSI is not now involved to any large extent in the investigation of UFO reports. However the decision mentioned in paragraph 2(c) above may still be valid. Possibly the matter should be considered further.

(E.A. Bernard) S/L

Classification cancelled / Changed to ....Unclas
By authority of ....DSIS
Date 25/6/84
Signature ....
Unit / Rank / Appointment ....NDSIS

eight is most curious, indicating that the Director of Air Intelligence was unaware of the policy mentioned in paragraphs two and three. Was DSI examining reports and withholding results? — *National Archives of Canada*

DEFENCE RESEARCH BOARD

Minutes of a Meeting to Discuss "Flying
Saucers" Sighting, 22 April, 1952.

Chairman: Dr. O.M. Solandt (DRB)

Present: S/L L.P.S. Bing (JIS)
                             F/L V.L. Bradley (DRB)
                             Col. G.M. Carrie (DRB)
                             G/C D.M. Edwards (DAI)
                             Mr. A.J. Langley (DRB)
                             Dr. P.M. Millman (Dom. Observ.)
                             Cdr.J.C. Pratt   (DNI)
                             Mr. W.B. Smith   (DOT)
                             Lt.Col. E.H. Webb (DMO & P)

Secretary: Mr. H. C. Oatway (DRB)

       The Chairman opened the meeting with
a brief reference to the more frequent occurance of
"Flying Saucer" sightings. The frequency and persis-
tency of the sightings would tend to discount the theory
of 'hallucinations'. This, coupled with an aroused
public interest in these sightings, tended to call for
a more active stand on the matter. At present the
gathering of reports was rather haphazard and the
reaction of the Services was passive. It is thought
that a more active and intensive effort should be made
to obtain these data on an organized basis, and all
reports investigated and analysed. The objects of
the meeting were then to determine if a more serious
effort is justified and, if so, ways and means of
implementing an organized effort. Organizations such
as the Observer Corps might be enlisted for the job
of sighting. If nothing else, this could serve as a
useful training for the Corps. An examination of the
theories might prove useful in giving a lead to the
best locations for sighting. It was fortunate that
proponents of the theories of terrestrial and extraterrestrial origins were in contact with the D.R.B.
and their data could be examined first hand.

       The Air Force representatives then
briefly outlined the work done by the USAF up to a
year or so ago. As these efforts consistently
resulted in 'nil returns' their project, in so far
as the press and public were concerned at least, had
been discontinued. Very recently, however, this investigation was re-opened , but is now classified.

       In the discussions which followed,
it was pointed out that precise and realistic details
were lacking in all known reports. If observers such
as the Rangers, watchers on ship board and the Observer Corps, which incidentally is really still in the
paper organization stage, are to be enlisted some
well planned guidance would be necessary. A small
booklet illustrating typical celestial phenomena
would result in more intelligent observation and
eliminate many erroneous impressions. It was considered desirable to obtain information from U.S.
interviews obtained under proper interrogation procedure, but to avoid the U.S. analysis of these

The minutes of the first meeting of what was to become Project Second Storey,
showing the Defence Research Board's (DRB) level of interest in UFOs. The
second paragraph indicates that the United States Air Force (USAF) was also
reopening classified investigations, though the press and public were told
otherwise. — *National Archives of Canada*

. B. Smith
..rtment Of Transport
Air Services, Telecommunications Div.
Ottawa, Ontario, Canada

Dear Mr. Smith:

January 14th. '54

Re: Flying Saucer, Or ..
Aeroform Research.

File 59-00-3

   This is in acknowledgment of your courteous letter of
Jan. 11, 1954, concerned with the above subject and, in reply to my letter of Jan. 5th. The reference file number of your last letter is 5200-3.

   In re to your reference to George Adamski and Desmond
Leslie, it may interest you to know that Dr. Layne (of the BSRA) and I
have been (and are) in collaborative contact with Leslie, Adamski, et al,
in the serious Saucer research circles for quite some time. We have, via
the BSRA releases, published Adamski's intimate reports and helped to interpret them, many months before the publication of the book "Flying Saucers Have Landed". I am in regular research collaborative contact with
Mr. Desmond Leslie and we correspond regularly. Dr. Layne and/or I have
had collaborative or co-operative contacts with other others of serious
"best seller" Saucer books, i.e. Ray Palmer, Kenneth Arnold, Frank Scully,
etc. and there is a more or less "inside story" to the writing and contents
of each such volume.

   I was in correspondence with Frank Scully and furnished
him with Saucer research data, about eight months before the appearance of
his book "Behind The Flying Saucers". Scully appears to have made the serious error, in his book, of attributing a good deal of the magnetic data
in our BSRA releases, to a mysterious (but, later, discredited Dr. "G")
altho this does not necessarily impair the authenticity and value of the
balance of his Saucer book, which more or less paved the way for others
of its kind.

   Dr. Layne and I are members of, and/or in co-operative
contact with the heads of several Saucer research organizations in the U.S.
and other countries, each of which makes some contribution to the Saucer
research picture, however minor. The BSRA was the first in the field nearly
seven years ago and has, by far, the most real and advanced research findings, as well as the most competent, scientifically and metaphysically
astut~ membership. I might add, however, that only a small, inner circle
of scientifically trained members take part in the most active and deeper
aspects of Saucer research. Of this group or inner circle, Dr. Layne has
been and is relying on this writer, for many if not most of the final interpretations of Saucer phenomena, as they come up or are reported from various
quarters. My studies and interpretations, I might add, are a balanced int-
egration of the scientific or objective side and the metaphysical or sub-
jective aspects of Saucer research. No other approach is possible or will
afford explanations that make sufficient sense, in terms of the many phenomena or Aeroforms and their behavior.

   The BSRA membership includes a hard, scientifically
alert core of professional scientists, physicists, chemists, electronic
experts, mathematicians, etc. all well versed in the borderland sciences.
We have had and have confidential research projects related to Saucers
and related phenomena, which would astound orthodox science. We have had
and have a deep and keen interest in the propulsive drives of Saucers, and
my BSRA and private files in that field is second to none and still growing.

(No.1)

This letter to Wilbert Smith from Borderland Sciences Research Associates (BSRA)
sheds some light on information contained in Scully's book, *Behind the Flying
Saucers*. Smith was intrigued with the psychic aspect of contact with UFOs.
— *National Archives of Canada*

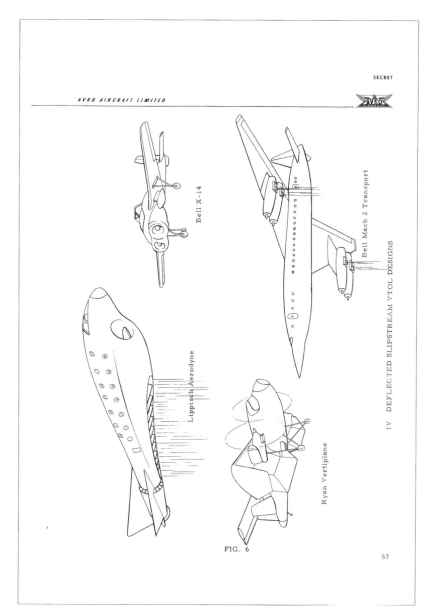

Bell X-14

Bell Mach 2 Transport

Lippisch Aerodyne

Ryan Vertiplane

IV DEFLECTED SLIPSTREAM VTOL DESIGNS

FIG. 6

Some interesting concepts being investigated by U.S. companies. Avro personnel were monitoring the work of these companies as their own work on the Avrocar progressed. — *Author's files*

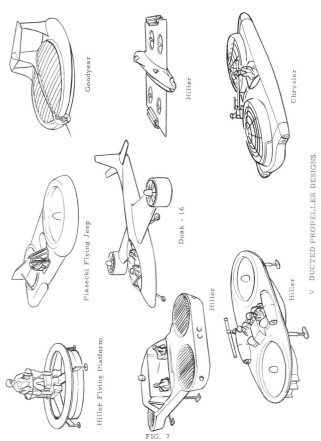

Goodyear

Hiller

Chrysler

Piasecki Flying Jeep

Doak - 16

Hiller Flying Platform

Hiller

Hiller

V   DUCTED PROPELLER DESIGNS

FIG. 7

V̇ 2000-4 (D Ops)

Canadian Forces Headquarters
Ottawa 4, Ontario.

ι7 November, 1967.

Mr. Warren Smith,
3808 17 St S.W.
Calgary, Alberta.

Dear Mr. Smith:

May I take this opportunity, on behalf of the Chief of
the Defence Staff, to thank you for providing the Department of
National Defence with the two excellent photographs of an unidentified
object.

The photographs were subjected to a detailed photo
analysis investigation, utilizing the descriptive information provided
with the photographs. The following findings were made:

(a) The object had a diamenter of some 40 to 50 feet
and a depth of 11.5 to 14 feet, giving a diameter/
depth ratio of approximately 4 to 1.

(b) The shadow detail in the photographs showing a roll
effect is more suggestive of a torus than an oblate
ellipsoid. The outside surface appears to lack
protrusions and highlight areas suggest a shiny,
bright surface.

Unfortunately, it has not been possible to identify or
explain the object shown in the two photographs. However, it may be
of interest to note that the Department of National Defence and other
interested agencies in UFOs have received a number of photographs of
unusual aerial sightings that can neither be identified nor explained.

Two enlarged coloured copies of the photographs in question
are enclosed herewith for your retention.

With your permission, it is intended to forward copies of
the coloured photographs to the University of Colorado for their study
and evaluation. As you may be aware, the United States Air Force has
selected the University of Colorado, under defence auspices, to under-
take an independent scientific study into UFOs.

Yours truly,

W.W. Turner
Colonel
for Chief of the Defence Staff

/C LP Robertson/2-5427/md
List
Ori
Circ

This letter explains DND findings on the Warren Smith photographs, noting that
a number of unexplained photographs have been received by DND. Where are
they? They were not in DND files or those of the NRC. — *National Archives of
Canada*

<u>MEMORANDUM</u>

V 1540-1 TD 8030 (D Ops)

February, 1968

To: SPECIAL ASSISTANT TO MND

MINISTERIAL INQUIRY
UNIDENTIFIED FLYING OBJECT —
MR. W.A. SMALL

Reference: A. V 2000-4 (D Ops) 17 November, 1967.

1. A technical assessment of the two photos taken by Mr. Warren Smith were subjected to a detailed analysis by the Defence Photographic Establishment. The conclusions arrived at by the Establishment were sent to Mr. Warren Smith Reference A.

2. At no time during the course of the investigation were lights of any type mentioned by Mr. Warren Smith, his two companions or the Photographic Establishment.

3. The possibility exists that the object might be a secret military project or some other type of terrestrial body but as it did not interfere with any military installations it does not pose a known threat to our national security. NRC and various universities have taken note of the sighting and may pursue the matter from a scientific aspect.

F.B. Caldwell
Commodore Secretary Defense
Staff

(W. Main) Maj
2-2900

A memo from Commodore Caldwell (Director Air Operations) to the Special Assistant to the Minister of National Defence. Paragraph three notes that Warren Smith might have seen a secret military project. [*Note*: This document was recreated from the original, which could not be clearly reproduced for publication.] — *National Archives of Canada*

20 Dec 76   20/5-5

Incident involving an unknown object trailing a refueling mission

405- Called by Maj Volmar 21st S.D. concerning an unknown object following a refueling mission involving 3 KC-135s (Camel 61, 62, 63) and one C-5. The object was observed visually and on radar from the KC-135s from 2147Z 16 Dec position 44°16'N 51°00'W to 2240Z 16 Dec at position 45°10'N 57°04W at which time object disappeared. We had no specials or unknowns in that area during that time period. I asked I.D. for all the information they had on this refueling mission.

426- Called by NCOC Col. Patterson concerning the above information. I asked why
755- it was almost 5 hours after the incident that this was reported by SAC, and why the aircraft did not use Alcc or Guard for our assistance. Col. Patterson directed me to save any tapes available for a reduction to see if a fourth aircraft could be observed at position 45°10'N 57°04'W at 2240Z 16 Dec.

580 - Maj Hall was called by me and asked what type of reduction would be necessary to secure the track, route and flight size of the 3 KC-135s from 162147Z to 162300Z. He suggested a SNAP for ID and then a Cy reduction of all tracks.

530- I D has given S.D. the following information:
   Since there was no incident reported at the time concerning this track I.D. had no record as to when it was made a friendly track. However, after checking back with moncton it was found that moncton picked up this track at 162222Z. I.D. estimates that this track was made a friendly after checking with moncton Amis on the flight plan of a track in this area at 2230. At 162301Z this track passed over Sydney. Also at this time a height cut of 26,000 and 27,000 feet was made of this flight of three aircraft. I.D. believes that this track was probably labeled M257 through M266. It is difficult to know exactly which track number was assigned because there was no special concern about the track at that time.   No F/P STAIRS   QM good ??? definition.

535- Col. Patterson was called and told the above story. I also directed SMC to save the tape from 2147Z 16 Dec to 2300Z 16 Dec saved for seven days for reduction.
Col. Patterson said that if our reduction reveals any information regarding an object following this flight, report such data to NCOC and refer to his

Notes from a 22nd NORAD region file. The UFO followed American refuelling aircraft but NORAD personnel did not learn of its existence until five hours after the incident, when it was officially reported by Strategic Air Command (SAC).
— *National Archives of Canada*

Command Director log Notation of 17/0418 entry.

UDDed Remarks: The visual sighting of the object trailing the KC135's was thought to be 500 to 1000 feet low and 1/2 mile in trail. The observations were made by the boom operator and the navigator of one of the KC-135's. Lights on object were reported to be much brighter than running lights on an aircraft.

Helen W. Jackson

NOTE

I contacted QM ARTCC watch supervisor (18 2030Z own) and requested information on any TKS flying within the vicinity of the KC135's during the the time frame of the report. The supervisor informed me that they did not have any flight strips for that particular area at the specified time. We talked with the controller for the mission and reiterated that he did not notice anything unusual about the flight.

The supervisor further stated that they have good track definition and were able to discern three separate aircraft and weather. Our computer print outs varify this, M259 was tracked through the system at FL 260. The positions and height coincides with the KC135. Our ident people remember the track and it came up automatic Friendly as it was squawking the correct MARK XII SIF code.

If something was there our Ground Environment systems did not register them. I discussed this with LCOL Richardson (4N 8W) and suggested that in the future if a situation like this occurs again their aircrew could give us a call on HFCc. We might pick something up on the Scope cameras.

20/12/76

Ralph Ly Capt
A OPS (W)
TOS

Notes

CHAPTER 1

1. Edward U. Condon, *Scientific Study of Unidentified Flying Objects*, E. P. Dutton & Co., Inc., New York, 1969
2. RG 97, Vol. 193
3. John Robert Colombo, *Mysterious Canada*, Doubleday Canada Limited, Toronto, 1988
4. Ibid.
5. Margaret Sachs and Earnest Jahn, *Celestial Passengers: UFOs & Space Travel*, Penguin Books, New York, 1977
6. C. A. Chant, "An Extraordinary Meteoric Display," *The Journal of the Royal Astronomical Society of Canada*, Vol. 7, No. 3, 1913
7. John Robert Colombo, *Mysterious Canada*, Doubleday Canada Limited, Toronto, 1988

8. Ibid.
9. Dwight Whalen, "Vanished Village Revisited," *Fate*, Llewellyn Publications, November 1976

CHAPTER 2

1. Notes by Wilbert Smith courtesy Arthur Bray
2. Renato Vesco, *Intercept UFO*, Grove Press Inc., New York, 1974
3. Ibid.
4. RG 24, Vol. 17988
5. Ibid.
6. Ibid.
7. Aime Michel, *The Truth About Flying Saucers*, Pyramid Books, New York, 1956
8. Timothy Good, *Above Top Secret*, Macmillan of Canada, Toronto, 1988
9. RG 97, Vol. 182, File 5010-4, Pts. 1-2
10. Ibid.
11. RG 24, Vol. 11982, File 1270.50
12. Notes by Wilbert Smith courtesy Arthur Bray
13. Ibid.
14. Ibid.

CHAPTER 3

1. RG 24, Vol. 17988
2. Notes by Wilbert Smith courtesy Arthur Bray
3. Ibid.
4. RG 97, Vol. 182, File 5010-4, Pt. 1
5. Aime Michel, *The Truth About Flying Saucers*, Pyramid Books, New York, 1956
6. RG 97, Vol. 182, File 5010-4, Pt. 1

7. Ibid.
8. Ibid.

CHAPTER 4

1. RG 24, Interim 49, Vol. 7523, Acc. 83-84/167, File 3800-10-1, Pt. 1
2. Ibid.
3. RG 24, Vol. 17988
4. RG 97, Vol. 115, File 5010-4
5. RG 24, Interim 49, Vol. 7523, Acc. 83-84/167, File 3800-10-1, Pt. 1
6. RG 24, Vol. 17988

CHAPTER 5

1. William B. Scott, "'Black World' Engineers, Scientists Encourage Using Highly Classified Technology for Civil Applications," *Aviation Week & Space Technology*, March 9, 1992
2. "Project Y: An All-Wing Supersonic Aeroplane," A. V. Roe, Records of Directorate Scientific Information Services, Department of National Defence
3. Timothy Good, *Alien Contact: Top Secret UFO Files Revealed*, William Morrow and Company, Inc., New York, 1993
4. "Takes Off Straight Up Report Malton 'Flying Saucer' to Do 1,500 MPH," *Toronto Daily Star*, February 11, 1953
5. J. C. M. Frost, "The Canadian Contribution to the Ground Cushion Story," *Canadian Aeronautical Journal*, October 1961
6. "Project Y2: Flat Vertical Take-Off Supersonic Gyroplane," A. V. Roe, 1954, from Directorate Scientific Information Services, Department of National Defence
7. Renato Vesco, *Intercept UFO*, Grove Press Inc., New York, 1974
8. J. C. M. Frost, "The Canadian Contribution to the Ground Cushion Story," *Canadian Aeronautical Journal*, October 1961

9. Ibid.
10. "Avrocar Flight Evaluation 270 921 AFSC," from Defense Technical Information Center, Virginia
11. "Denial and Disinformation," *Jane's Defense Weekly*, Jane's Information Group Ltd., Alexandria, VA, December 12, 1992
12. "TR-AC-47, Joint ATIC-WADC Report on Project Silver Bug," Project No. 9961, February 15, 1955. Declassified March 29, 1995
13. Ibid.
14. Correspondence from Major George Filer (retired)

CHAPTER 6

1. Prime Minister Lester B. Pearson, on receiving the Nobel Peace Prize in Oslo, Norway, December 11, 1957
2. Timothy Good, *Above Top Secret*, Macmillan of Canada, Toronto, 1988
3. RG 97, Vol. 115, File 5010-4
4. RG 24, Vol. 17988, File S-940-105, Pts. 1-3
5. RG 24, Interim 49, Vol. 7523, Acc. 83-84/167, File 3800-10-1, Pt. 1

CHAPTER 7

1. RG 24, Vol. 17988
2. Ibid.
3. Ibid.
4. RG 77, Vol. 311, File DND/UAR 201-214
5. RG 77, Vol. 310, File DND/UAR 126-137
6. Ibid.
7. RG 24, Interim 49, Acc. 83-84/167, Vol. 7523, File DRB S 3800-10-1, Pt. 1
8. Ibid.
9. Ibid.

10. RG 97, Vol. 355, Engineering Group General Objectives of Rocket Launchings

CHAPTER 8

1. Edward U. Condon, *Scientific Study of Unidentified Flying Objects*, E. P. Dutton & Co., Inc., New York, 1969
2. RG 18, Vol. 5053, File DG-085-7-1
3. Ibid.
4. Ibid.
5. Ibid.
6. RG 24, Interim 49, Vol. 7523, Acc. 83-84/167, File 3800-10-1, Pt. 1
7. Ibid.
8. Ibid.
9. RG 77, Vol. 311, File DND/UAR 200
10. RG 18, Vol. 5053, File DG-085-7-1
11. RG 77, Vol. 316, File DND/UAR 126-137

CHAPTER 9

1. Dr. J. Allen Hynek, *The Hynek UFO Report*, Dell Publishing Co., New York, 1977
2. RG 24/184/167, Vol. 43, File 22NR-2075-5, Pt. 1
3. "Airmiss Report No. 2/95," *Commercial Air Transport Airmiss Reports (January-April 1995)*, Civil Aviation Authority Press Office
4. Ibid.

CHAPTER 10

1. "Air Force Order on 'Saucers' Cited," Vice Admiral R. H.

Hillenkoetter (retired), former director of the Central Intelligence Agency, quoted in the *New York Times*, February 28, 1960

2. Dr. J. Allen Hynek, *The Hynek UFO Report*, Dell Publishing Co. Ltd., New York, 1977

3. Edward U. Condon, *Scientific Study of Unidentified Flying Objects*, E. P. Dutton & Co., Inc., New York, 1969

4. Harvey Weinstein, *Father, Son, and CIA*, Formac Publishing Co. Ltd., Halifax, 1990

5. RG 24, Vol. 17988, File S-940-105, Pts. 1-3

6. Timothy Good, *Above Top Secret*, Macmillan of Canada, Toronto, 1988

7. "Air Force Report Shoots Down UFO Theories About 1947 Crash," *Ottawa Citizen*, September 18, 1994

8. Ibid.

9. "Denial and Disinformation," *Jane's Defense Weekly*, Jane's Information Group Ltd., Alexandria, VA, December 12, 1992

10. "Report of Air Force Research Regarding 'The Roswell Incident,'" Department of the Air Force, Air Force Public Affairs, September 8, 1994

CHAPTER 11

1. John Morton Blum, *V Was for Victory: Politics and American Culture During World War II*, Harcourt, Brace Jovanovich, New York, 1976

2. Ibid.

3. J. Bronskill, "Canada's 'X-Files' Soon May Become Ex-files . . . Hmm," *Ottawa Citizen*, July 27, 1996

Bibliography

BOOKS

Barnett, Frank R. *Political Warfare and Psychological Operations: Rethinking the U.S. Approach.* National Defense University Press with National Strategy Information Center, 1989.

Berlitz, Charles, and William Moore. *The Roswell Incident.* London: Granada Publishing, 1980.

Blum, Howard. *Out There.* New York: Simon and Schuster, 1990.

Blum, John Morton. "Victory, Limits of American Internationalism." Chap. 9 in *V Was for Victory: Politics and American Culture During World War II.* New York: Harcourt, Brace Jovanovich, 1976.

Blum, Ralph, and Judy Blum. *Beyond Earth: Man's Contact with UFOs.* New York: Bantam Books, 1974.

Bray, Arthur. *The UFO Connection.* Ottawa: Jupiter Publishing, 1979.

Campagna, Palmiro. *Storms of Controversy: The Secret Avro Arrow Files Revealed.* Toronto: Stoddart Publishing, 1992.

Colombo, John Robert. *Mysterious Canada.* Toronto: Doubleday Canada, 1988.

_____. *UFOs over Canada.* Willowdale, Ontario: Hounslow Press, 1991.

Condon, Edward U. *Scientific Study of Unidentified Flying Objects.* New York: E. P. Dutton & Co., 1969.

Edwards, Frank. *Flying Saucers — Here And Now.* Toronto: Bantam Books, 1967.

_____. *Flying Saucers: Serious Business.* Toronto: Bantam Books, 1966.

Emenegger, Robert. *UFOs Past, Present, and Future.* New York: Ballantine Books, 1974.

Friedman, Stanton. *Crash at Corona.* New York: Paragon House, 1992.

_____. *Top Secret/Majic.* New York: Marlowe & Company, 1996.

Fuller, John G. *Aliens in the Skies.* New York: G. P. Putnam's Sons, 1969.

Good, Timothy. *Above Top Secret.* Toronto: Macmillan of Canada, 1988.

_____. *Alien Contact: Top Secret UFO Files Revealed.* New York: William Morrow and Company, 1993.

Hynek, Dr. Allen J. *The Hynek UFO Report.* Ottawa: Dell Publishing, 1979.

_____. *The UFO Experience.* New York: Ballantine Books, 1972.

Keyhoe, Donald E. *Flying Saucers: Top Secret.* New York: G. P. Putnam's Sons, 1960.

Lorenzen, Coral E. *The Shadow of the Unknown.* New York: 1970.

Lorenzen, Coral, and Jim Lorenzen. *Flying Saucer Occupants.* Toronto: Signet Books, 1967.

_____. *UFOs Over the Americas.* Toronto: Signet Books, 1968.

Lusar, Rudolf. *German Secret Weapons of the Second World War.* New York: Philosophical Library, 1959.

Michel, Aime. *The Truth About Flying Saucers.* New York: Pyramid Books, 1956.

Peebles, Curtis. *Watch the Skies*. Washington: Smithsonian Institution Press, 1994.

Randle, Kevin D., and Donald R. Schmitt. *The Truth About the UFO Crash at Roswell*. New York: M. Evans & Co., 1994.

Rich, Ben R., and Leo Janos. *Skunk Works*. New York: Little, Brown and Company, 1994.

Sachs, Margaret, and Ernest Jahn. *Celestial Passengers: UFOs and Space Travel*. New York: Penguin Books, 1977.

Smith, Wilbert B. *The New Science*. Ottawa: Keith Press, 1978.

Spencer, John, and Hilary Evans. *Phenomenon: Forty Years of Flying Saucers*. New York: Avon Books, 1989.

Steiger, Brad. *Project Blue Book*. New York: Ballantine Books, 1976.

Steinman, William S. *UFO Crash at Aztec: A Well Kept Secret*. Boulder, CO: Wendelle C. Stevens, America West Distributions, 1986.

Trench, Brinsley Le Poer. *The Flying Saucer Story*. New York: Ace Books, 1966.

Vesco, Renato. *Intercept UFO*. New York: Grove Press, 1974.

Weinstein, Harvey. *Father, Son, and CIA*. Halifax: Formac Publishing, 1990.

Wilkins, H. T. *Flying Saucers Uncensored*. New York: Pyramid Books, 1955.

ARTICLES

"Air Force Order on 'Saucers' Cited." *New York Times*, February 28, 1960.

"Air Force Report Shoots Down UFO Theories About 1947 Crash." *Ottawa Citizen*, September 18, 1994.

Anselmo, Joseph C. "Life on Mars? Evidence Emerges." *Aviation Week & Space Technology*, August 12, 1996.

Bronskill, Jim. "Canada's 'X-Files' Soon May Become Ex-files . . . Hmm." *Ottawa Citizen*, July 27, 1996.

"Can't Close Our Minds on UFOs – Military Chief." *North Bay (Ontario) Nugget*, December 6, 1975.

Chant, C. A. "An Extraordinary Meteoric Display." *The Journal of the Royal Astronomical Society of Canada* 7, no. 3, 1913.

Dane, Abe. "Flying Saucers: The Real Story." *Popular Mechanics*, January 1995.

"Denial and Disinformation." *Jane's Defense Weekly*, December 12, 1992.

Douglass, Robert G. "Flying Saucers from Canada." *Invention & Technology*, Winter 1996.

Ferrell, K. "The Alien." *Penthouse*, September 1996.

"Flying Saucers with Colored Lights Puzzle N.S. Village." *Toronto Star*, October 12, 1968.

Frost, J. C. M. "The Canadian Contribution to the Ground Cushion Story." *Canadian Aeronautical Journal*, October 1961.

Fulghum, David. "Secret Flights in 1980s Tested Stealth Recon." *Aviation Week & Space Technology*, May 6, 1996.

Grescoe Paul. "This Man Knows UFOs." *Canadian Magazine, (Toronto) Star Weekly*, May 25-June 8, 1968.

Hartanto, Ruth. "UFO Expert Is Convinced Tape No Hoax." *Carp Valley (Ontario) Press*, February 4, 1993.

Hughes, David. "NASA Pilots Test Windowless Cockpit." *Aviation Week & Space Technology*, March 11, 1996.

Kennedy, Mark. "Strange Sightings in Canadian Skies." *Ottawa Citizen*, November 27, 1993.

Mr. X. "The Phantom Invasion of 1915." *Early Canadian Life*, May 1979.

"Multiple Sightings of Secret Aircraft Hint at New Propulsion, Airframe Designs." *Aviation Week & Space Technology*, October 1, 1990.

"Mystery of UFO Baffles Aviation Authorities." *Ottawa Citizen*, February 4, 1996.

"Nuclear Reactor: Aircraft Propulsion Reactor." *Encyclopaedia Britannica* 13, 1973.

Pratt, Bob. "Air Defense Chiefs Admit: We Tracked UFO on Radar and Scrambled Fighter Jets to Intercept." *National Enquirer*, August 1976.

Rutkowski, Chris. "The Falcon Lake Incident." *Flying Saucer Review* 27, nos. 1, 2, 3, 1981.

"Saucer Seeker." *Time*, November 23, 1953.

Scott, William B. "'Black World' Engineers, Scientists Encourage Using Highly Classified Technology for Civil Applications." *Aviation Week & Space Technology*, March 9, 1992.

_____. "New Evidence Bolsters Reports of Secret, High-Speed Aircraft." *Aviation Week & Space Technology*, May 11, 1992.

_____. "Scientists' and Engineers' Dreams Taking to Skies as 'Black' Aircraft." *Aviation Week & Space Technology*, December 24, 1990.

"Secret Advanced Vehicles Demonstrate Technologies for Future Military Use." *Aviation Week & Space Technology*, October 1, 1990.

"Space Sightings." *Maclean's*, January 29, 1996.

Stevenson, William. "Takes Off Straight Up Report Malton 'Flying Saucer' to Do 1,500 MPH." *Toronto Daily Star*, February 11, 1953.

Sweetman, Bill. "Hypersonic Aurora: A Secret Dawning." *Jane's Defense Weekly*, December 1992.

_____. "Secret Mach 6 Spy Plane." *Popular Science*, March 1993.

"Use Geiger Counter . . . Duhamel Circles Still a Mystery." *Camrose (Alberta) Canadian*, August 16, 1967.

Whalen, Dwight. "Vanished Village Revisited." *Fate*, November 1976.

REPORTS

"Airmiss Report No. 2/95." *Commercial Air Transport Airmiss Reports (January-April 1995)*. Civil Aviation Authority Press Office.

"AUFORA News Update Issue 02.06.96." AUFORA Web: http://ume.med.ucalgary.ca/aufora/

"Avrocar Flight Evaluation 270 921 AFSC." Defense Technical Information Center, Virginia.

"Project Y: An All-Wing Supersonic Aeroplane." A. V. Roe, Records of Directorate Scientific Information Services, Department of National Defence, Ottawa.

"Project Y2: Flat Vertical Take-Off Supersonic Gyroplane." A. V. Roe, 1954, from Directorate Scientific Information Services, Department of National Defence, Ottawa.

"Report of Air Force Research Regarding 'The Roswell Incident.'" Department of the Air Force, Air Force Public Affairs, September 8, 1994.

"Results of a Search for Records Concerning the 1947 Crash Near Roswell, New Mexico." General Accounting Office, GAO/NSIAD-95-187, July 1995.

"TR-AC-47, Joint ATIC-WADC Report on Project Silver Bug." Project No. 9961, February 15, 1955.

CANADIAN ARCHIVAL RECORDS

"Intelligence Sightings of Unknown Objects, 1947-1964." RG 24, Vol. 17984, File S-940-5, Pts. 1-2.

"Intelligence Sightings of Unknown Objects, 1950-1964." RG 24, Vol. 17988, File S-940-105, Pts. 1-2.

"Intelligence Sightings of Unknown Objects Outside Canada, 1950-1952." RG 24, Vol. 17988, File S-940-105-3.

"Air Services – Sightings of Unidentified Aerial Objects – Project Second Storey, 1952-1953." RG 97, Vol. 115, File 5010-4.

"Space Research and Satellites, UFOs, 1953-1966." RG 97, Vol. 182, File 5010-4, Pts. 1-2.

"Space Research and Technology, 1959-1964." RG 97, Vol. 104, File 5010-1, Pts. 1-3.

"Engineering Group General Objectives of Rocket Launchings." RG 97, Vol. 355.

"Counter Intelligence – Flying Saucer, 1952-1957." RG 24, Vol. 22349, File 9150-4.

"Target Detection – Search – Flying Saucers – General, 1950-1967."
RG 24, Int. 49, Acc. 83-84/167, Box 7523, File DRBS 3800-10-1, Pt. 1.

"UFO Sightings, 1965-1981." RG 77, Reels T-1741 to T1744. These
records extend to the present but not all are on microfilm.

"Engineering Group – General – Public Observation of Rocket
Launchings." RG 77, Acc. 83-84/355, Box 6, File 7700-7, DND –
V2000-4, Pts. 1-5.

"Intelligence Reports UFOs." RG 24, G10(F), Acc. 94-95/506, Box 1,
File C-2075-5, Pt. 1.

"Intelligence Reports UFOs." RG 24, G10(G), Acc. 84-85/167, Box 43,
2075-5, and Vol. 43, File 22NR-2075-5, Pt. 1.

RG 24, Acc. 1983-84/167, Box 7318, File DRB S-0300-3, Pts. 1, 2.

RG 12, Vol. 3280, File 5008-LWV.

RG 24, Vol. 20054, File Avrocar.

"NRC UFOs." RG 77, Vol. 311, DND/UAR 200. There is an entire
series in the Vol. 300 series, mostly on microfilm.

"NRC UFOs." RG 18, Vol. 3779, File HQ-400-Q-5.

Stefan Michalak RCMP file. RG 18, Vol. 5059, File DG-085-7-1.

RG 24, Int. 18, Vol. 17991, File 5949-119.

RG 24, Acc. 94-95/506, Vol. 1, File 2075.5, Interim File 230.

RG 24, Vol. 11982, File 1270.50 (Bremner Atomic Powered Aircraft).

RG 24, Vol. 4243, File O. M. Solandt – Correspondence w/Crawford
Gordon Jr. 1952-1956.

RG 24, Acc. 83-84/165 Vol. 59, File 9150-4.

Index